TACTICAL GENIUS
IN BATTLE

Simon Goodenough

TACTICAL GENIUS IN BATTLE

Edited and introduced by LEN DEIGHTON

PHAIDON

**Designed and edited for
Phaidon Press by
Berkeley Publishers Ltd,
9 Warwick Court,
London WC1R 5DJ**

© 1979 Phaidon Press Limited,
Littlegate House, St Ebbe's Street,
Oxford

Published in the United States of
America by E. P. Dutton, New
York

First Published 1979

ISBN 0 7148 1949 2
Library of Congress Catalog Card
Number: 79–88938

Printed in Great Britain
by Fakenham Press Limited,
Fakenham, Norfolk

Contents

Introduction
by LEN DEIGHTON

War, or the threat of it, has been with us all our lives and remains our greatest problem. Strange, then, that the serious study of war and its causes is still regarded as a rather perverse and not-to-be-encouraged pursuit. My own interest in the subject began after graduation from the Royal College of Art. Seven years as a full time student had made me feel a great need to see the real world. The simplest way to do that was to become an air steward with British Airways and during that time my off-duty hours were devoted to a self-inflicted reading programme of geography and history, designed to help me understand the world through which I was flying at such a hectic rate.

At the end of the year I concluded that the history of warfare was the 'cement' of which the walls of history were built. Wars evidenced the social changes that preceded them and marked the technological skills that so often decided them. For instance, in the first decade of this century, European life remained virtually unchanged but the men and machines of 1918 were radically different from those of 1914. Even more changed were the Americans after their civil war of the previous century. That war began as a rural conflict but by the time the fighting ended America had begun to turn into an industrial super power.

The arguments that in the past have led to war are discovered again and again in histories, and differ little from those that separate today's enemies. One analysis of the history of warfare, by the American sociologist Pitirim Sorokin, estimated that since the Norman conquest England had been at war for more than fifty years of each century. Russia's record was only marginally better than that, and Spain had spent even more time at war.

Liddell Hart's theories of war, expressed carefully in his many books, began with the thought that wars are linked to economics. He went on to modify these ideas and link war with psychology. Eventually he concluded that war was 'personal' in the sense that it was an expression of the attitudes of men in power. My study of military history supports that theory.

War seems to be a reflection of those societies that engage in it. One sees, too, a curious interchange that affects both combatants. Prolonged warfare causes each nation to resemble its enemy. In its simplest form we see this when uniformed armies engage guerrilla forces; the irregulars adopt military ranks, titles and badges while the regulars create informal battle groups and blacken their faces.

Although battle is a confrontation of technologies, the skill of the general is not a science and certainly not an art. Generalship most resembles that curious game played by children of many nations in which two opponents extend hands to resemble flat paper, scissors or a fist of rock. Paper wraps, and so defeats a rock but is cut by the scissors; these in turn can be blunted by the rock. So battle consists of the skill and luck in bringing to the fore the weaponry that defeats the enemy. When history records an army unprepared, it seldom refers to a force unready for battle but rather to men who have prepared to meet some different sort of opponent.

Carl von Clausewitz said that no human activity was so influenced by chance as was war: perhaps he had never heard of love. Napoleon sought lucky men for his commands but was likely to bear in mind the way in which fortune favours the bold. He knew that young colonels would bring daring to a battle, while elderly generals, with reputation made and rank secure, would play safe. More young French colonels at the battle of Waterloo would probably have changed the outcome of the fight.

Complex weapons and the supply problems created by them have changed

Supply lines, camp and cannon—a 16th-Century battle scene.

the nature of warfare. In early wars supply was simply a matter of how many missiles a foot soldier could carry on to the battlefield and few battles continued after sundown. Now the military clerk's pen is mightier that the sword. When in 1914 the German Emperor wanted to march against Russia and leave France neutral, he was told that this was impossible. The paper work, long since completed, provided no such alternative. The First World War began and swallowed Europe's millions.

It was not easy to choose which military ideas should be included here. Not all the good ideas resulted in triumph. Some were doomed to failure. Erich Manstein, widely regarded as the finest military brain of this century, designed the extraordinary German attack upon France in May, 1940. Yet his achievements in extricating German armies from the Red Army's great assaults were even more brilliant. Neither should it be forgotten that one of the Royal Navy's greatest triumphs was due to Admiral Ramsay's men and women clerks who made the Dunkirk evacuation only marginally less than a miracle.

Of course, it is tempting to give disproportionate attention to twentieth-century battles. What historian can deny the attraction of such a wealth of written material, together with film, photo and living eye-witnesses? This especially applies to the gigantic battles of the Eastern front and the war in the Pacific which still provide a great deal of work for future historical study.

As we go back in time, conclusions become more tentative. History has always been the memoirs of the victors and as we look at the ancient accounts of battle we have to accept them for what they are: over-dramatized stories from second-hand sources motivated by a need for propaganda. Yet it is these old

A 19th-Century version of an army line-up from Roman times.

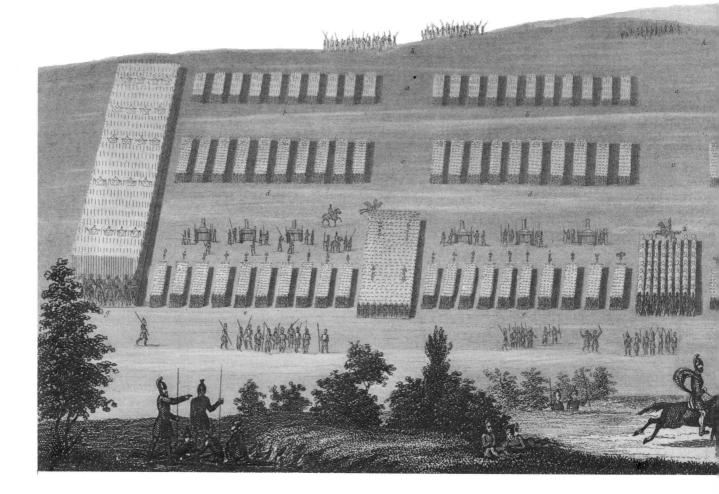

tales that hold pride of place in any history of warfare. It is not hard to understand why. Quite apart from their literary appeal we find in them simplified drama and some element of wisdom. Perhaps the wise men are not always good men, but surely it is this triumph of ideas over brute force that makes the student of military history return constantly to his maps and notes.

In this book, the battles selected for study have been sufficiently analysed to enable a comparison of tactical ideas to be made. The same ideas may occur again and again but always the results are different, not only because of the way in which they may be combined but also because of the personality and intelligence of the commanders.

Hilaire Belloc (in *The Tactics and Strategy of the Great Duke of Marlborough* published by Arrowsmith in 1933) defined tactics as the manoeuvre of men after contact with the enemy. Strategy, he said, is concerned with bringing armies into action in a fashion best calculated to give them advantage. And yet it is not so easy to divide these two tasks. All too often the battle is both strategic and tactical and the great commanders are men who have enough authority to create a tactical advantage within the strategic intention.

I suppose it could be said that true tactical genius is best demonstrated by subordinate commanders acting within the narrow confines of their allotted tasks. The question arises, how would some of history's greatest soldiers have fared under the command of a Hitler or a Churchill? Indeed, we hope that one of the pleasures of this book will lie in enabling the reader to join in the historian's great game of 'if'.

The Tactical Themes
by SIMON GOODENOUGH

War is a complex and cruel affair. There is no survival for the weak, the irresolute or the confused. 'Find me officers who will fight,' ordered MacArthur, when his troops fell back before the Japanese, entrenched in the jungle at Buna. This book is about the determination to fight and the tactics employed to bring the enemy to battle and to ensure victory.

We have chosen twenty-seven battles spread over more than 3000 years and in many different countries to highlight the tactical genius of the commanders who won those victories. These examples demonstrate the climax of each battle. They reveal the cunning and skill with which twenty-seven great leaders succeeded in outwitting and outfighting their opponents in an extraordinary range of situations. There are some battles that are world famous, such as Napoleon's victory at Austerlitz or the German invasion of France in 1940. There are some that are less well-known, such as Johan Baner's brilliant Swedish victory at Wittstock.

In each case, the initiative and resolve of the commander have played a decisive part in the ultimate success. Sometimes he has been able to exploit his enemy's unforced error (Marathon and Yom Kippur); at other times he has had to trick his enemy into a vulnerable position (Leuthen and Meiktila). Sometimes he has been able to dictate the place and manner of the battle (Salamis and Mohi Heath); at other times he has made instant decisions to seize chance opportunities (Rocroi and Gaugamela). In every case, he has won by making the best use of his resources and by showing a positive willingness to fight. The battles we have chosen demonstrate his skill in command.

Tactical cunning makes strange bedfellows of battles that may be centuries apart. We have not described them in chronological order. It is often the unexpected juxtaposition of two apparently dissimilar battles that throws new light on both. The victors of ancient Cannae and 20th-Century Tannenberg each achieved a double-envelopment of their enemy's flanks. An enticement similar to that which Wellington successfully offered the French at Salamanca very nearly brought about the destruction of Ramesses II at Kadesh. The dogged persistence of Grant at Vicksburg was matched by MacArthur's forceful determination in the face of great difficulties at Buna. Of course, there are many factors that make each battle absolutely different (the armies, equipment, conditions and attitudes of the time) and the protagonists themselves are rarely conscious of the contrasts and parallels we have drawn but a rough pattern of repeated problems and solutions does appear.

Basically, there are only about three ways of attacking the enemy: from in front, from the side or from behind. All other tactical preliminaries are directed at preparing for one or more of these approaches. The frontal attack may be at the enemy's strongest point (Leuctra) or it may penetrate a weak gap. This gap may already exist (Battle of France) or it may have to be created by a tactical ruse (Gaugamela). The attack on the side, or flank, may be done openly (Buna) or by surprise (Garigliano). The enemy may also be attacked on both flanks simultaneously (Tannenberg) and in the rear (Cannae) for a complete encirclement. In modern warfare, the enemy can, of course, be attacked from above, by aircraft, but this is usually achieved in conjunction with ground troops. Guerrilla troops avoid a battle-front situation and, if possible, attack from within.

We have started the book with some examples of direct assaults on the front of the enemy line and then moved on to some successful penetrations, flanking attacks, surprise flanking attacks and, finally, encirclements. At the beginning of each battle, there is a paragraph in italics which explains how the battle fits into the pattern and what are the factors that make it similar to, as well as different from, the battles before it in the book. It is helpful to read these paragraphs first to understand the theme of the book.

No categorization can be followed too closely. There are frequently strong underlying cross-currents in the form of the tactical ploys and resources with which the commander prepares for, and by which he achieves, his attack. For example, the feigned withdrawal reappears in one form or another at Hastings, Mohi Heath, Austerlitz, Kadesh, Salamanca and Salamis, to give opportunities for various lines of attack. The oblique advance enabled the Thebans at Leuctra to make a direct attack against the strongest part of the Spartan line; it enabled Frederick to turn the Austrian flank at Leuthen; and it enabled Alexander to penetrate the Persian line at Gaugamela.

Frederick made a feint attack at Leuthen to distract the Austrians from his real attack. The feint attack reappears at Wittstock, Meiktila, Vicksburg and El Alamein, in different guises and with varying degrees of success. One important purpose of the feint is to persuade the enemy to commit his reserves. This purpose is based on the sound theory that the side which can produce the last reserve at the crucial moment is likely to win. A great commander will therefore create new reserves whenever possible in preparation for a new line of attack. He will often have to accomplish this by withdrawing troops from the line as soon as he has committed his previous reserve. This ploy was used with marked success by Montgomery at El Alamein and by Pilsudski at Warsaw. The introduction of a reserve force at the critical point played a vital part in many battles, including Kadesh (a lucky chance), Gaugamela, Salamanca, Breitenfeld, Pharsalus, Leuthen, Rocroi and Daras.

Any commander's greatest tactical weapon is surprise. Almost all the battles in this book contain at least some element of surprise, whether because of the directness, or deviousness, of the attack. There are three possible approaches. The most perfect is to catch the enemy completely unawares (Garigliano). It is also possible to tire the enemy out by keeping him constantly guessing the next move (Vicksburg). The third approach offers the enemy something positive to distract his attention from the real purpose of his opponent—a feint attack (Leuthen) or a holding operation (Austerlitz). The greatest weakness of the commander who does not take the initiative, either in planning or attack, lies in his continual search for something, or indeed anything, to which to react. He is therefore vulnerable to the ploys of his opponent.

After the German defeat at El Alamein, General Thoma expressed the view that, 'In modern warfare the tactics are not the main thing. The decisive factor is the organization of one's resources—to maintain the momentum.' The organization and proper deployment of resources have always been complementary to tactical skill. The Mongols understood this in the 13th Century. Much later, both Marlborough and Napoleon achieved remarkable feats of organization in their separate advances along the Rhine and across the Danube. Speed of manoeuvre (Austerlitz, France and Mohi Heath), flexibility in defence and offence (Daras, Gaugamela and Yom Kippur) and firepower (Blenheim, Breitenfeld and Salamanca) are also important tactical complements.

In addition, the commander who has trained his troops to obey orders instantly and with perfect synchronization can be sure that the vital tactical decisions he makes on the battlefield will be put into effect. The creation and proper use of a competent, and often innovative, army is obviously an asset to tactical planning. Both Alexander and Frederick benefited at key moments during their battles from the disciplined training of their troops. The model army of Gustavus Adolphus provided an irresistible combination of forces at Breitenfeld and so did the *Blitzkrieg* tactics of the Germans in 1940. Even at

Hastings, it was the cunning combination of cavalry and bowmen that ulti-
mately gave victory to William of Normandy. Wellington's thin red line at
Salamanca and the Mongol's single cavalry arm at Mohi Heath were both used
with devastating effect. The lesson to be learned was that every commander
should know the strengths and weaknesses of his own army and that he should
be able to protect its weaknesses and make the maximum use of its strengths.
Cannae, Daras and Leuctra are good examples.

The tactical turning point is more obvious in ancient battles than in modern
ones. In earlier centuries the numbers involved were usually smaller and the
battles lasted for hours rather than days. The battles generally assumed a
discernible pattern over which the commander exerted direct personal control.
In modern warfare whole groups of armies may be involved in battles lasting
weeks or even months. Attrition often seems to be the main aim, whereby each
side attempts to wear out his opponent. We have chosen battles in which there
can still be seen some of our main themes coming through the larger-scale, and
the more obscure, conditions. Buna is a modern example of a relatively small
battle but the conditions in which it was fought stretched the action over 3–4
months. The conflict was dogged and wearying rather than dramatic but our

tactical themes do still emerge: a steady flanking attack and a determined commander.

We have given a short description of the campaign that led up to each battle and a brief biography of the commander. Obviously, there has been space to include only some of the tactical triumphs of warfare but we have given two naval battles (Salamis and Cape St Vincent) because they neatly demonstrate tactical problems and solutions that parallel those on land. No commander has more than one of his battles included, however brilliant his other victories may have been. Many famous battles and commanders have had to be left out.

It is the commander who dominates the story. Pilsudski sits alone all night in his library planning how to push the Russians back from Warsaw. Hoffman anticipates Ludendorff's plan to trap Samsonov's army at Tannenberg. Manstein prepares the way for Guderian to drive a wedge through the Ardennes so deep that even Hitler cries halt. Grant grimly explores every bog and bayou to outflank the Confederates in Vicksburg. Themistocles tricks his own reluctant colleagues into battle with the Persians. Every example has its story and its character. They are stories not only of tactical inspiration but of strong and resolute personalities.

A battle scene from the 18th Century—in this case Bohemia.

The simplest tactic in warfare is the direct attack against the enemy's front. This was modified when opposing armies each strengthened their own right wing in an attempt to turn the enemy's left wing. In the first truly original tactic in history, the brilliant Theban commander, Epaminondas, advanced in an oblique line to concentrate his force against the powerful Spartan army at its strongest point, while 'refusing' his weaker wing. His bold attack achieved surprise and a remarkable victory.

Epaminondas, whose highly original tactics brought about the defeat of the Spartans at Leuctra.

The rivalry between Athens, Sparta and Thebes, the three main Greek city states, produced a confusion of alliances that swung first one way and then another. These alliances were made still more confusing by the intervention of Persia, who supported first Athens and then Sparta. In 394 BC, a Spartan fleet was defeated by an alliance of the Persians and Athenians. In the same year, a Spartan army was victorious against the Thebans and Athenians. A general peace was established between Athens and Sparta in 371 BC. This time Thebes was the odd man out. The Theban citadel had been occupied by the Spartans 10 years before and the citizens were not prepared to put themselves at risk again by breaking up their protective unification of surrounding Boeotia to comply with the demands of the two senior allies. Undefeated as yet on land, the Spartans decided to take positive action to 'persuade' Thebes to do what they wanted.

They marched with an army of 10,000 from the Peloponnese across the isthmus and into Boeotia, where they were met by a determined force of about half their number of Thebans and Theban allies. The Greek armies had learned from the Persian wars of the previous century to extend their cavalry and missile arms. There were horsemen from Thessaly and bowmen from Crete on the Theban side. The Spartans also had a cavalry arm but still relied heavily on their solid phalanx formation. It was with this that they hoped to perform the traditional tactic of turning the Theban left wing with their own reinforced right wing. One unwelcome result of this tactic could be that both armies simply wheeled round as their right wings pressed forward, but the Spartans did not envisage this occurring on the plain by the village of Leuctra. They were confident in their ability to hold the anticipated attack on their own left while they smashed the Theban left with their picked troops. The Spartan king, Cleombrotus, led the Spartans on the right and spread his allies to the left.

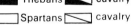

▮ Thebans	◣ cavalry
▯ Spartans	◪ cavalry

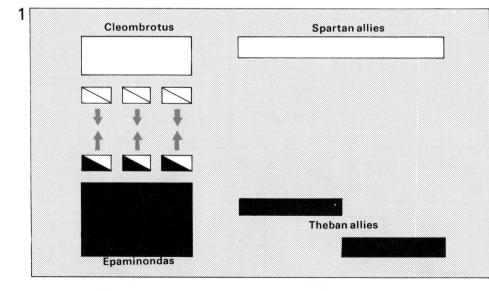

Epaminondas concentrates his force against the Spartan right wing and advances in an oblique line so that he might save his own weak right from the first onslaught.

Epaminondas was painfully aware that he had a considerably smaller force than the Spartans, that his own allies were almost certainly undependable and that his opponents had a reputation for invincibility second to none. He knew just how easily Cleombrotus could break through his own left wing and how difficult he himself would find it to turn the Peloponnesian left. There was obviously no point in doing what Cleombrotus expected him to do in the traditional way. He decided to oppose the Spartan right with maximum strength and to try to keep his vulnerable allies out of the fight (Plan 1).

Cleombrotus had massed his Spartan right in a phalanx twelve-men deep. Epaminondas placed his Thebans in the phalanx forty-eight-men deep and, in front of these, he placed his well-trained cavalry. He put his allies on his right in a half-hearted hope that, in a crisis, they might be able to hold the Peloponnesian left while the Thebans struck against the right. To protect the allies from an immediate engagement and to concentrate his forces against Cleombrotus,

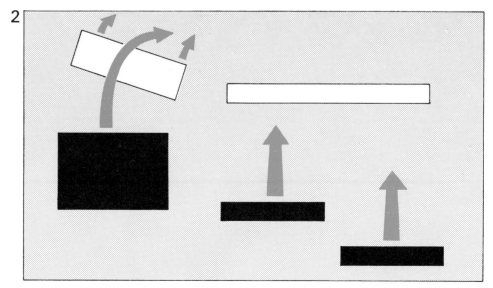

2

Taken by surprise by the unexpectedly strong attack on their own strongest wing, the Spartans are pushed back and the battle is won before the Theban weakness is put to the test.

the Theban commander then advanced in an oblique line, with his strong left wing moving ahead of the rest of the army. The cavalry units of the two armies met first in a preliminary skirmish in which the better-disciplined Theban horse managed to drive the Spartan horse from the plain. But that action in no way determined the outcome of the battle itself. The main engagement was between the Spartan and Theban infantry.

An essential aspect of any tactic is to achieve surprise. The 'art' of warfare begins when something is attempted beyond the mere collision of opposites on a predetermined course. Considerations of numbers and firepower can be overruled by the heightening of morale among the attackers and the lowering of morale among those who have been surprised. The question of morale plays a large part in the outcome of any battle. Epaminondas achieved surprise with his tactics at Leuctra.

The Spartans were tough, ruthless soldiers, brought up in the hardest possible training ground, and they were confident in the strength of their phalanx. But their twelve ranks appeared meagre before the forty-eight ranks of the Thebans and they were unable to sustain the sheer weight of the Theban attack (Plan 2). They had never expected the Thebans to risk the mass of their smaller force in one desperate throw against the Spartan right. Slowly, but surely, they were pressed back and forced onto the centre of the Peloponnesian army, unable to use their weapons properly in the resulting crush. Their courage was unavailing. They were cut down rank by rank and routed before any serious engagement began on the other wing.

More than 2000 soldiers were killed among the Peloponnesians. These included Cleombrotus himself and 700 Spartans. The rest of the army fled in panic but the Thebans were unable to pursue at once because they did not trust their allies. They could not be sure just how they would behave once the Thebans' backs were turned. In fact, there was little need for a pursuit. The Spartan reputation for invincibility on land was destroyed and the battle of Leuctra heralded the decline of Spartan supremacy in Greece.

The importance of Leuctra in tactical terms was quite as great as in political terms. The skill of Epaminondas demonstrated how battles could be won not merely by brute strength but by the cunning application of strength at the right point. Epaminondas took a considerable risk in concentrating his force and, thereby, depleting the rest of his already weaker line. His gamble was a

Above: The reverses of two silver staters from Tarsus, about 400 BC, showing Greek hoplites defending themselves with spear and shield. (By kind permission of the Trustees of the British Museum)

Opposite top: A silver tetradrachm, signed by the artist Eukleidas, of about 410 BC. The obverse shows a quadriga, or four-horse chariot, of the type that might have been used at Leuctra. The charioteer is being crowned by Nike, the winged Victory. (By kind permission of the Trustees of the British Museum)

Opposite: Typical arrowheads from the 5th and 4th centuries BC. An attacking force was most vulnerable to bowmen as they were advancing and before they came to close quarters.

dangerous one but he played it firmly and without reservation. That was the measure of his genius.

One man who studied the tactical methods of Epaminondas was Philip of Macedonia, who spent three years as a hostage in Thebes. Greatly impressed by the Theban commander, he returned to his own country and forged a combined army of infantry, cavalry and artillery, with which he united Greece under one rule and with which his son, Alexander, swept away the Persian empire. Later in this book, we shall find how Alexander himself made brilliant use of the oblique tactic first demonstrated by Epaminondas. We shall also see how another commander, many centuries later, proved that time had not devalued the tactic: Frederick the Great of Prussia used it with stunning effect at the battle of Leuthen.

Although Epaminondas was unable to pursue the Spartan army at once, he showed strategical good-sense when he marched south to the Spartan home-land of Laconia, the following year, and freed Messenia and Arcadia from Spartan influence. In this way, he was able to balance Spartan power in the Peloponnese. Subsequently, he began to build a Theban fleet to increase the power of Thebes at sea as well as on land. Athens and Sparta, ever-jealous, reactivated their alliance and once again attacked. In 362 BC, their combined armies were defeated at the battle of Mantinea by the already proven oblique approach of the Thebans, but Epaminondas himself was wounded in the action and died subsequently. The Thebans never regained their impetus.

Epaminondas (c. 418–362 BC)

The dominance of Thebes as a land-power in Greece was almost solely due to the influence of Epaminondas. He fell victim to the rivalry of his colleagues and was deprived of his command after his victory at Leuctra and his campaign in the Peloponnese. He became a common soldier in Thessaly but was recalled because the Thebans could not do without him. He led two more campaigns against the Spartans but his death at Mantinea virtually negated the benefits of victory. His main achievements were the overthrow of Spartan predominance and the introduction of tactical originality as characterized by the oblique attack. He did not achieve any lasting power for Thebes. Despite his period of disfavour, he was considered to be a man of excellent character and reputation.

Like the Thebans at Leuctra, William of Normandy found himself forced to make a direct attack against a confident and strongly-arrayed enemy. His approach to the problem was very different and his tactical solution more cunning than that of Epaminondas. Unable to make headway in the first clash of arms, he feigned withdrawal and then counter-attacked his misguided pursuers with marked success. A combined force of Norman cavalry and bowmen finally cracked the courageous but tiring Saxon housecarles.

William I, King of England and Duke of Normandy, from a two-sceptres type coin of 1074–77. (By kind permission of the Trustees of the British Museum)

There were three claimants to the throne of England when King Edward the Confessor died in London on January 5, 1066. The first to proclaim himself king was Harold Godwinson, Earl of Wessex. This was contested by Duke William of Normandy, who considered that he was the sole rightful heir. Two years before, Harold had been tricked into forgoing his own claim by an oath made in gratitude for being rescued from shipwreck by William. Angry that Harold had ignored his oath, William made careful preparations during the spring and summer for an invasion of England and received the Pope's blessing for his enterprise.

Harold took sensible precautions against this threat. He mobilized an army along the south coast and sent a large fleet to patrol the Channel. William was ready to sail in early August but was delayed several weeks by bad weather. The delay was too long for Harold, who had to order his fleet back to London for resupplying. It was then that the third claimant arrived, the King of Norway, Harald III Hardraade, with the support of Harold Godwinson's exiled brother, Tostig. Harald's Vikings routed the Earls of Mercia and Northumbria at Fulford, near York on September 20. Within five days, King Harold had hastened north with his nucleus of professional soldiers, the housecarles, and what local militia (fyrdmen) he could gather on the way. He caught the Vikings by surprise at Stamford Bridge. Harald Hardraade and Tostig were both killed and the raiders totally defeated.

Unfortunately for King Harold, his problems had only just begun. With the English fleet out of the way, William had made an unopposed landing on the night of September 27 at Pevensey, near Hastings. Harold heard the news a few days later and immediately marched south. He covered the 190 miles (304 kilometres) to London, with his housecarles, in four days. Ordering up what-

Normans ▮ archers ⬧⬧⬧⬧
Saxons ▯ cavalry ⬙

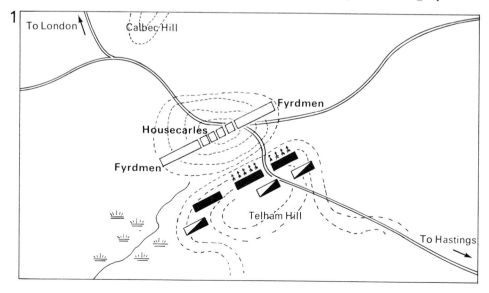

Harold's housecarles are flanked by fyrdmen as the Saxons take up their defensive position on the hill. Confident of their strength, they were nonetheless tired and were caught by surprise by William's rapid advance.

RA NCI: INPRELIO

The Saxons drive the Norman cavalry back from their assault on the slope, from the Bayeux Tapestry. This could be the moment of feigned retreat but the Norman cavalry look to be in serious trouble.

ever local militia he could in the south, he hastened on to meet William and camped at Calbec Hill, about 6–7 miles (10–11 kilometres) from the Norman camp at Hastings. The hill dominated the main route to London and the 'hoar apple tree' that stood there was a well-known local landmark.

Harold's haste to come to grips with William was a strategical error that probably lost him his kingdom. He should have bided his time and let the Normans tire themselves out. But he was flushed with victory in the north, he was confident that his housecarles were the best infantry in Europe and he was angered by William's devastation of the Wessex countryside. (Marlborough similarly tried to provoke his opponent by destroying the countryside before Blenheim.) He had also to bring about an early battle because his fyrdmen had a service of only 40 days. On the other side, it was very much in William's interests to fight quickly: the English fleet were once more in the Channel, his

The Norman left is driven back down the hill and some of the Saxons break rank to pursue the Normans. On this occasion the Saxons returned to their line. When the cavalry on the Norman right made a feigned withdrawal, the Saxon left was not so lucky. They pursued and were caught when the Normans turned to attack them.

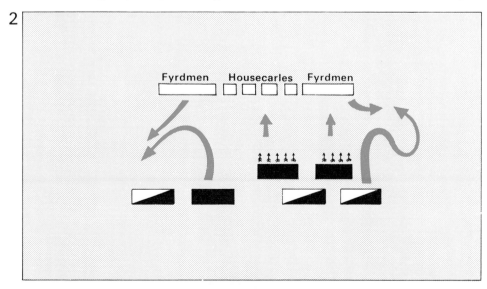

feudal levies would soon get bored and the longer the battle was delayed the longer Harold would have to raise more soldiers.

In his determination to attack, William very nearly caught Harold by surprise. He made a rapid advance early on the morning of October 14 and prepared his forces on the slope of Telham Hill, opposite the ridge in front of Calbec Hill. A small stream and some marshy ground ran down to the west between the two slopes. Harold's position provided a good natural defence. The ridge was about 700 yards (640 metres) long, with steep enough slopes on either side to guard against flank attacks. Harold placed his army in a solid phalanx, with his trained bodyguard of housecarles around him in the centre and his fyrdmen stretched to either side. If anything, the ridge was a little too short. The Saxons were packed closely together, which helped to solidify the shield-wall but made them a perfect target for William's archers (Plan 1).

The housecarles were armed with two-edged swords and great Danish axes. They were protected by tough, wooden shields, metal helmets (if they could afford them) and varying degrees of mail. The fyrdmen were armed with a variety of clubs, staves, swords, axes, javelins and stone hammers. Many of them had arrived only the night before and were very tired. There were no archers (although they had proved useful at Stamford Bridge) and no cavalry. Although the housecarles travelled on horseback, they fought in the traditional way on foot. In all, there were about 2000 housecarles and about 5000–6000 fyrdmen.

William had both cavalry and bowmen. He drew up his army in three lines: archers to the front, infantry next and cavalry behind. The cavalry, protected by chain mail, were armed with lances, swords, axes and maces. They did not charge all together but galloped up to the enemy in small groups or singly, threw their lances from a distance and then attacked with sword and mace. The infantry were armed with spears and most of the archers used the short bow. There were about 2000 knights and nearly 6000 bowmen and spearmen. The opposing forces were therefore roughly equal.

The battle opened at about nine o'clock, when William sent forward his archers to fire up the slope at the Saxon line. This had little effect on the shields of the housecarles. It was followed by a massed attack of Norman spearmen accompanied by some of the cavalry, who could do little against the great Saxon axes. The spearmen rushed back down the hill and caused considerable confusion among the cavalry behind them as both groups floundered in the marshy ground. For a moment, the Normans seemed to be on the run and several of the untrained Saxon fyrdmen started down the hill in pursuit (Plan 2). It was then

Typical weapons and armour of the time of the Battle of Hastings, taken from the Bayeux Tapestry.

The Saxons are in full retreat, broken at last by the combined attack of the Norman bowmen and cavalry, from the Bayeux Tapestry.

that a rumour spread among the Normans that William himself had been hit.

The Duke at once removed his helmet to prove to his soldiers that he was alive and well. He reasserted his control over the battle and rallied his left wing. The Saxon infantry faltered in the muddy ground, the pursuit withdrew and the battle regained its former equilibrium. William tried once more to make a direct attack on the housecarles, in which he himself took a leading part. The fighting was fierce but the attack was repulsed. It was probably then that William tried his first intentional feigned retreat, hoping to repeat the previously unplanned method of drawing the Saxons down the hill. The cavalry on William's right turned as if to flee, the Saxon left took the bait and when they reached the bottom of the slope the Normans turned again and charged them with great effect (Plan 2).

This did not decide the battle, although it certainly had a demoralizing effect on the Saxons. The housecarles remained steadfast throughout the afternoon. It was quite a different tactical ruse that introduced the closing phase of the day. William ordered a combined attack by the cavalry and the bowmen. The bowmen advanced rapidly, then paused to fire their arrows high in the air so that they rained down on top of the Saxons. (This was the moment when, according to popular myth, Harold was struck in the eye.) Then the cavalry charged *en masse* (for the first time) through the ranks of the bowmen and hit the Saxons before they had properly recovered from the hail of arrows (Plan 3). There followed a long struggle, during which Harold was killed by a Norman spearman, and the housecarles eventually broke and scattered.

William's victory won him the throne of England. His feigned withdrawal and his clever use of combined forces in the final assault were examples of tactical dexterity that were successfully repeated by other great commanders.

Duke William of Normandy (c. *1027/28–1087*)

William became Duke when he was 9 and there were 12 years of anarchy before he established control over his dukedom. He visited England in 1051 and may well have received a promise of the English throne from his kinsman, Edward the Confessor. His invasion of England and his victory at Hastings were followed by his coronation at Westminster Abbey on Christmas Day, 1066, but it took him another 5 years to assert his authority over the whole country. He died of an injury while on campaign in France and was buried at Caen. Known to us as William the Conqueror, the first of a long line of Norman kings, he had a powerful personality and his military tactics were marked by determination and cool calculation.

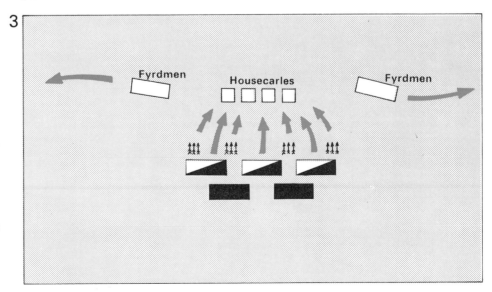

3

In the final phase of the battle, the Norman archers fire a devastating hail of arrows, which is followed up by a determined charge by the Norman cavalry. The Saxon fyrdmen abandon the battle and the housecarles are eventually broken.

The Duke of Marlborough demonstrated yet another variation on the direct attack when he defeated Marshall Tallard. Confronted by a French army which had established the best of its veteran infantry in and around the defensible villages of Blenheim and Oberglau, he chose to make his first advance directly against those points and seized the chance to bottle up the enemy in their own strongholds. He then pushed between the two villages to drive off the rest of the French and complete his victory.

John Churchill, Duke of Marlborough, whose victory at Blenheim was well-rewarded by his country.

The Battle of Blenheim was the first great French reverse for about fifty years. It secured Marlborough's reputation and the reputation of the British soldier in Europe. It saved Vienna from being overrun by the French and it denied Louis XIV his ambition of dominating Europe. The War of the Spanish Succession, in which Blenheim played a key part, was the struggle to stop a power-block between France and Spain on the death of the last of the Spanish Habsburgs, the mentally unstable Charles II. The considerable resources of France, Spain and Bavaria were opposed by the Grand Alliance formed in 1701 between Great Britain, Holland, Austria, Prussia, Hanover, Portugal and Savoy. The theatre of war ranged from Spain and northern Italy to southern Germany and the Netherlands.

By 1703, the French had a series of strong fortresses in the Spanish Netherlands and were threatening to join up with the Bavarians in the east and take Vienna. If they achieved that, then they could concentrate their attentions on the Allies to the north and west of their border. They had the advantage of interior lines of communication and it was believed that no army could march east to relieve Vienna without being taken in the flank by the French as it advanced along the course of the Rhine. Marlborough, as Captain-General of the Anglo-Dutch forces, decided the march was possible. He determined to save Vienna and proceeded to make meticulous preparations for a trek of nearly 300 miles (480 kilometres), concentrating simultaneously on providing adequate supplies and clothing for his troops on the way and on deceiving the enemy as to his real intentions. This remarkable march was an example of administrative genius admired by military historians ever since (Plan 1).

Arrangements were made with German bankers for the money to pay for all necessities (so that no ally would be alienated by the passage of the army), spare equipment was sent ahead by river to await the arrival of the army at various

■	British and Allies
▨	cavalry
□	French and Allies
▨	cavalry

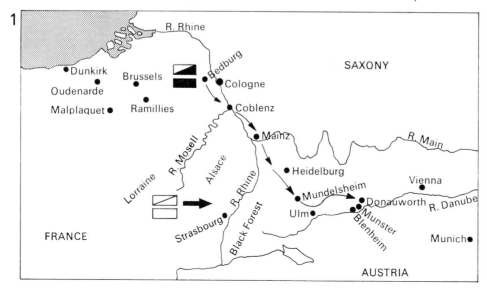

1

R. Rhine
Dunkirk
Brussels
Bedburg
Cologne
SAXONY
Oudenarde
Ramillies
Coblenz
Malplaquet
R. Mosell
Mainz
R. Main
Lorraine
Alsace
Heidelburg
Vienna
R. Rhine
Mundelsheim
Donauworth
R. Danube
Ulm
Munster
Blenheim
Strasbourg
Black Forest
FRANCE
Munich
AUSTRIA

The route of Marlborough's surprise march from Bedburg to the Danube, to save Vienna from the French. He feinted first towards the Moselle and then towards Alsace before striking east. His bold move enabled him to get between the French army and Vienna.

A print of 1735, showing the capture of Marshall Tallard and the French cavalry being pursued across the River Danube.

points and, just before the army reached Bavaria, there were new boots waiting for every soldier. Marlborough made as if to turn down the Moselle to attack France but, when he reached Coblenz, he hastened on along the Rhine. Then he made as if to attack Alsace but turned suddenly away from the Rhine and marched for the Danube. Only then did his enemies realize his true objective.

Before he reached the Danube, at Ulm, Marlborough's army of 40,000 was joined by Prince Eugene of Savoy and Prince Lewis of Baden. Prince Eugene turned to keep a watchful eye on Marshall Tallard's army hastening from France, while Marlborough concentrated on trying to make the Elector of

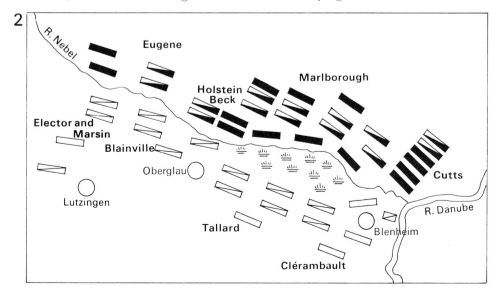

The positions of the armies before Blenheim. The opening of the battle was delayed until Prince Eugene had reached his place on Marlborough's right wing.

Bavaria come over to his side. Marlborough's first aim was to get between the Elector's army and Vienna and he saw the key to this move in the town of Donauworth and its formidably fortified hill known as the Schellenberg. The storming of the Schellenberg, on July 2, was a desperate and costly affair but it clearly demonstrated that a determined attack against the enemy's strongest point could achieve surprise and success. This was to become a favourite tactic of Marlborough's. It did not, however, persuade the Elector to join him.

There followed a frustrating period in which Marlborough set about a thorough devastation of the Bavarian countryside in an effort to apply further pressure to the Elector, who bided his time awaiting the arrival of the French army. His patience paid off. Eugene steadily retreated before Tallard's advance and, in early August, Tallard and the Elector joined forces. On August 12, they camped at Blenheim, on the north bank of the Danube. Marlborough and Eugene had by that time also rejoined and were camped at Munster, about 5 miles (8 kilometres) downstream, between Blenheim and Donauworth. The French held an apparently strong position at Blenheim and were more concerned with reaching Vienna than in fighting a battle. They did not expect Marlborough to attack and they knew that part of his force, under Prince Lewis, was temporarily absent. Marlborough, on the other hand, was delighted at the chance to take positive action at last. On the morning of August 13, he made a rapid advance to the north-east bank of the small tributary, River Nebel. From the far bank, Tallard looked in amazement as the morning mists lifted at about nine o'clock to reveal the approach of an army he had believed to be in retreat.

Tallard and the Elector had about 56,000 men and ninety guns between them. Tallard's main force was spread along a two-mile (3 kilometres) front between the villages of Blenheim and Oberglau. There were twenty-seven battalions on his right wing, under Clérambault (eleven of these were actually inside Blenheim), and fifteen battalions around Oberglau, under Blainville. Tallard took the centre, between the two villages, with most of his cavalry and the nine remaining battalions. He had virtually no cavalry on his extreme right, where he relied on the Danube to protect his flank. On his left flank, the Elector formed up his own force between the villages of Oberglau and Lutzingen (Plan 2).

Marlborough's total strength, including Eugene's force, was about 52,000 with about sixty guns. Marlborough himself took the centre, Lord Cutts took the left wing, opposite Blenheim, and Eugene marched along the bank of the Nebel to face the Elector, on the extreme right. Marlborough realized that the main battle was going to be fought on his left and centre, against the French, but it was essential that Eugene simultaneously tied down the Elector's troops so that they could not reinforce Tallard. The Marshall's intention was clearly to attack Marlborough's centre as he advanced up through the marshy ground on the French side of the river. He would charge first with his cavalry and then make flanking attacks with his infantry from Blenheim and Oberglau. Marlborough's tactical solution to this trap was to hold back from his centre and surprise the French by directly attacking their strongest points. If he could contain the bulk of the French infantry within the two villages, he would then be at a considerable numerical advantage in the centre.

His plan was an inspired assessment of the situation and made the best possible use of several elements in his favour. Firstly, there was surprise, whose morale-boosting effect, although not dramatic in this case, should not be underestimated. Secondly, there was the failure of Tallard to stand close enough to the river so that he could frustrate Marlborough's crossing. Tallard had made two more mistakes. His worst was to handicap his infantry by restricting them to the environs of the villages, where they could not move freely. This was a weak, defensive measure. He also failed to provide adequate infantry support for his cavalry in the centre.

On top of this, Marlborough had certain advantages in the equipment and training of the soldiers under his command. The French cavalry still fought in the caracole style, charging, firing and turning away to reload. Marlborough's cavalry had been trained in the style of Gustavus's Swedish cavalry, to advance three-deep at the trot, building up speed until they hit the enemy in a concerted attack with their swords. Marlborough also knew how to make the best use of the recently introduced flintlock and ring bayonet (replacing the matchlock and plug bayonet) to increase the firepower of his troops in linear formations and hollow squares. (The plug bayonet had fitted into the actual barrel so that no shots could be fired once the bayonet was fitted. The ring bayonet fitted over the barrel so that the gun could still be fired.)

Eugene did not reach his position until noon. There was an intervening artillery barrage from either side during which Marlborough's engineers prepared bridges for crossing the river. Cutts's brigades advanced against Blenheim, holding their fire until the last possible moment. As many as a third of the first brigade never had a chance to fire at all. They were mown down by the French muskets. But their places were filled and the attack continued. Alarmed by its progress and energy, Clérambault ordered up all his reserves and crammed them into the village to fend off the British. This was not only unimaginative but it played directly into Marlborough's hands. Twenty-one French battalions were trapped in Blenheim and, to all intents and purposes, out of the battle so long as Cutts could hold them there. Those were his orders. There was no need to take or enter the village yet (Plan 3).

Marlborough turned his attention to Oberglau, where the Prince of Holstein-Beck was leading a charge of ten battalions of infantry against the French garrison. The Marquis of Blainville checked his attack and turned him back to the Nebel. There followed push and counter-push around Oberglau while Marlborough was moving the infantry of his centre across the river and through the marshy ground on the south-west side. This would have been the ideal moment for Tallard to make a concerted attack but it was Marsin, who had been fighting with the Elector against Eugene, who saw the opportunity, not Tallard. Just after two o'clock, he made a cavalry charge against the right flank of Marlborough's centre to split the centre and Holstein-Beck's hard-pressed wing (Plan 3).

This was the testing moment of the battle, which brought out Marlborough's coolness and the confidence that inspired not only his men but also his fellow-commanders. He sent urgently to Eugene for reinforcements. Eugene himself was in a dangerous situation at that time, trying to hold a force considerably

Previous page: A near-contemporary print of the Battle of Blenheim. It shows the Danube on the left and the French forces already shut in the villages of Blenheim and Oberglau.

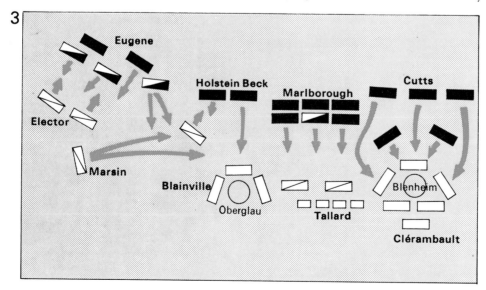

3

On Marlborough's left, Cutts traps the French in Blenheim. On his right, Holstein-Beck attacks Oberglau and, on the extreme right, Eugene advances against the Elector. As Marsin threatens to charge Marlborough's flank, Eugene sends help and the crisis is averted. Marlborough's centre safely crosses the stream.

larger than his own, but he recognized that Marlborough would not have made the request without very good reason and he instantly dispatched a cavalry force sufficient to turn the tables against Marsin's flanking attack. Holstein-Beck followed this up with a renewed infantry assault and, within a short time, Blainville, like Clérambault, was shut up in his own village.

Marlborough paused before the final blow, to reorganize his troops. An hour later, with ninety squadrons of cavalry and twenty-three battalions of infantry, he launched his attack on Tallard's centre of sixty cavalry squadrons and nine raw infantry battalions (Plan 4). Checked at first, Marlborough's cavalry then charged in a solid mass, which nothing could withstand. Tallard looked desperately to his right for reserves but they were all inside Blenheim. He sent for reinforcements to the Elector on his left but the Elector was by now under pressure from Eugene, who threatened to outflank him around Lutzingen. Unlike Eugene, the Elector would not risk helping his fellow-commander.

Lord Orkney, in the centre, having helped to clear the field, turned left and completed the encirclement of Blenheim. Clérambault fled and was drowned in the Danube. Tallard was captured. By evening, the officers in Blenheim had surrendered and the Elector had withdrawn from the battle. Marlborough suffered 12,000 killed and wounded; the French casualties numbered 20,000, as well as 14,000 prisoners and sixty guns. The Duke wrote to his wife, Sarah, on the back of a tavern bill: 'I have not time to say more but to beg you will give my duty to the Queen [Anne] and let her know Her Army has had a Glorious Victory. Monsieur Tallard and two other Generals are in my coach and I am following the rest.'

The Duke of Marlborough (1650–1722)

John Churchill's army career advanced rapidly but his fortunes at court fluctuated with changing allegiances under James II, William of Orange and Queen Anne. He became Captain-General of the English Army on Anne's accession and Commander-in-Chief of the United Armies of England and Holland. He won a series of brilliant victories, beginning with Blenheim (for which he was amply rewarded) and followed by Ramillies (1706), Oudenarde (1708) and the less successful Malplaquet (1709). Intrigues at home forced him to stay abroad for the last 2 years of Anne's reign and, when he returned to England, he played little part in public life. He was a skilful diplomat and a charming and intelligent man. He took as much care over the comfort of his soldiers as over the details of military planning. He also had the clarity of mind to adapt to a crisis, as Blenheim aptly demonstrated.

4

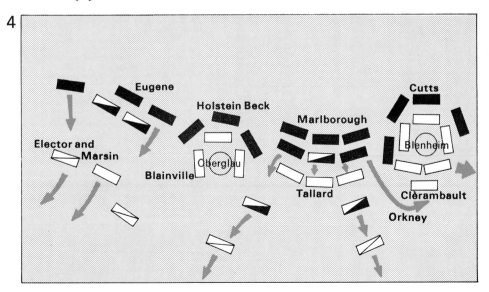

With the French securely held in Blenheim and Oberglau, Marlborough attacks the French centre and drives it from the field. On Marlborough's right, the Elector withdraws under pressure from Eugene; on the left, the encirclement of Blenheim is completed.

Austerlitz 1805

Napoleon repeated Marlborough's dramatic forced march along the Rhine and across to the Danube almost a century later. But when he confronted the combined Russian and Austrian army he used guile to avoid a direct attack. Luring the Russians down from their dominant position on the Pratzen Heights, he penetrated the gap between the two allies, seized the Heights himself and attacked the Russians in flank and rear from their own stronghold.

Napoleon proclaimed himself Emperor of the French at the end of 1804. In the same year he collected together a vast army at Boulogne in preparation for an invasion of England. 'If we can control the Channel for six hours,' he said, 'we will be masters of the world.' Before his preparations

Left: Napoleon Bonaparte, victor of Austerlitz and one of history's greatest commanders. (The Parker Gallery, London)

Below: Napoleon overlooks the battle of Austerlitz, directing the carefully planned tactics that outmanoeuvred the Russians and Austrians.

were complete, he was compelled to turn his attention eastwards, where Russia and Austria were building up a concentration of force. Together with Britain, they were the major partners in the Third Coalition against Napoleon. The Austrians, under General Mack, had marched west into Bohemia; two Russian armies were marching south to join the Austrians and a second Austrian army was returning from Italy. Napoleon turned his Grand Army about and marched east to the Danube to meet this powerful challenge. Like Marlborough, he made precise plans for the march and ensured that provisions and suitable camp sites were carefully prepared ahead. He moved as fast as possible, to strike his enemies before they assembled in force (Plan 1).

By early October 1805, Napoleon had marched north of the Austrian army at Ulm and deceived them as to his real destination. He turned abruptly south, behind Ulm, and cut the Austrians off from their communications with Vienna. General Mack proved indecisive in the face of this dilemma. After ten days of being encircled by Napoleon's army, he surrendered on October 20 with nearly

30,000 men. It was an almost bloodless victory for Napoleon but it was only the opening move in his 'Moravian' campaign. Prussia was by then threatening to join the Allies with yet another army and winter was rapidly closing in. Napoleon's troops were tiring and he had to force a battle soon.

By this time, the Russian commander, Kutuzov, had between 50,000 and 60,000 men as far south as the Danube, with another 30,000 waiting to join him, under Buxhowden, in Moravia. Napoleon pressed forward in an attempt to encircle them and cut off their line of retreat, just as he had with General Mack, but Kutuzov was a great deal more cunning than Mack. He steadily withdrew in front of the French army, forcing Napoleon to march deeper and deeper into hostile territory. In mid-November, Napoleon seized Vienna. At the same time he received news of Nelson's victory at Trafalgar the previous month. In the light of his current problems, he regarded Trafalgar as a relatively minor setback.

The Russians and remaining Austrians were by then encamped at Olmutz, under the command of Tsar Alexander I and the Emperor Francis I. (The Battle of Austerlitz is sometimes known as the Battle of the Three Emperors.) They had about 80,000 or 90,000 men between them and were expecting their numbers to be more than doubled by the Austrians from Italy and by the Prussians. Napoleon reached Brunn with 53,000 and immediately prepared his trap to lure the Russians into battle before their reinforcements arrived and before the morale of his Grand Army was lowered beyond recall.

His first concern was to deceive the enemy as to his real intentions. Having advanced from Brunn, he then began to withdraw. First he requested an armistice, then he retreated in apparent confusion, leaving the town of Auster-litz to the Russians and abandoning also the vantage point on the Heights around the tiny village of Pratzen, just to the west of Austerlitz. He also deceived them as to his strength. Although he had only 53,000 men with him in the front line at the end of November (and that was all the Russians could see), he had a reserve under Davout and Bernadotte of another 20,000 or more within a day or two's march behind him. It was Napoleon's practice to advance through enemy country on as wide a front as possible to spread the burden of subsistence, but, by speedy manoeuvre, he was able to concentrate his forces at whatever point he wanted in the event of battle. Austerlitz proved the effectiveness of these tactics.

Confident that Napoleon was on the run, the Russians massed their infantry on the Heights of Pratzen, under Buxhowden, believing that they would easily be able to sweep away Napoleon's apparently weakened right wing and cut off

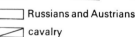

■ French	◢ cavalry
□ Russians and Austrians	
◿ cavalry	

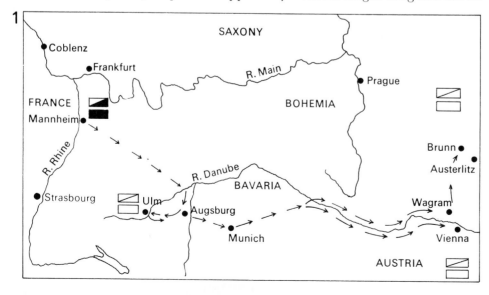

Napoleon repeats Marlborough's swift march to the Danube, to attack his enemies before they assemble in force. On the way he surrounds General Mack in Ulm before marching on to Vienna and Austerlitz.

The dead and the dying lie underfoot as Napoleon receives news of the progress of the battle.

his lines of communication with Vienna. Napoleon deliberately encouraged this belief by placing a relatively small force on his right. He knew that Davout should probably appear in time to take the strain on that wing when the Russians attacked. Napoleon's main force, largely unseen by the Russians and Austrians, was in the centre, under Soult, ready to charge up to the Pratzen Heights and divide the Austro-Russian army as soon as the Russians had committed themselves on their left. On his other wing, Napoleon was relying on a holding operation. Lannes' infantry and the cavalry of Murat, later to be supported by the arrival of Bernadotte, faced the infantry of Bagration and the cavalry of Prince Liechtenstein. This wing covered the main road from Brunn to Olmutz and was protected by the Mountains of Moravia to the north. On the south wing of the two armies, there was marshland and several lakes. The Goldbach stream ran between the opponents, with the French to the west and the Allies to the east (Plan 2).

Despite the peril of their situation, the French were vastly cheered by the confidence of their Emperor, who explained his plan of action to them. The morale of the soldiers was further raised by an incident on the night before the battle, the night of December 1. It was not known whether the fire was accidental or whether some brands were lit on purpose, but there was a sudden

The Russians and Austrians face the French across the Goldbach stream. Buxhowden holds the Pratzen Heights but cannot see the full strength of Napoleon's centre, under Soult. The Russians were more concerned with cutting round Napoleon's apparently weak right wing to sever his link with Vienna.

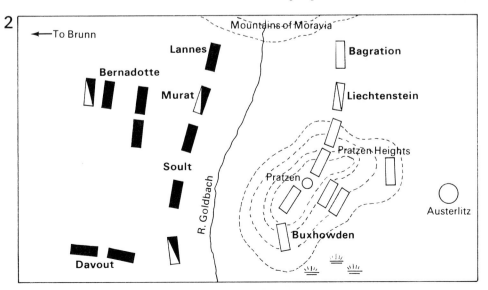

outburst of flame accompanied by a spontaneous acclamation of the Emperor when word went round that the next day was the anniversary of his coronation. In the Russian camp, the Tsar was equally eager for battle and overruled the caution of General Kutuzov, who would have sensibly preferred to wait until the arrival of the expected reinforcements.

The action opened early on the morning of December 2, before the mists of dawn had cleared. Bernadotte had already joined up with Napoleon's left, bringing the French forces up to 65,000. Davout was still moving up to his position. The first stage of the battle was exactly as Napoleon had planned (Plan 3). Buxhowden took the bait and advanced in strength, down from the Pratzen plateau, to attack the vulnerable-looking French right. This was the moment of risk for, until Davout arrived, the French flank was greatly outnumbered and hard pressed. It was a calculated risk and, as usual, Napoleon's timing was perfect. Davout leant his weight to the French resistance and by dint of determined fighting they held Buxhowden.

At about nine o'clock, Napoleon launched his counter-attack, under Soult. The infantry of the centre stormed up the Pratzen slope to the top, which was by then virtually clear of the main Russian force. Unaware of the strength of the French centre, the remaining Russians were taken by surprise. There followed two hours of fierce fighting on the Heights, during which the Russian Guards counter-attacked the French and were themselves driven off by Napoleon's reserve infantry. It was a classic example of the timely use of a reserve. By about eleven o'clock, the Heights were securely in French hands and the cavalry were pushing on to the Allied headquarters in Austerlitz.

The battle to the north was less dramatic but nonetheless successful for the French. Lannes managed to hold Bagration's attack and stopped his attempt to turn his flank. Murat's cavalry resisted the charge of Prince Liechtenstein's horse and drove them from the field, thus cutting the Allied right off from its centre (Plan 4). Feeling the weight of the steadily increasing pressure, Bagration was compelled to pull back his troops and to start a withdrawal. It was time for Napoleon to turn his full attention on the southern flank, where Davout was still holding the bulk of the Russian infantry.

Bernadotte was left on the Heights to hold them against any further counter-attacks. The remainder of the French centre then marched down the slope, crossed behind Buxhowden's rear and took him in the flank (Plan 4). It was a hopeless situation for the Russians. Attacked from almost every side, Buxhowden's wing was doomed. He himself, with some of his troops, managed to fight his way out. Many others fled south across the marshes and lakes and

A double-barrelled flintlock rifle of French manufacture, 1805, the year of Austerlitz. It lies complete in its case with all its original accessories.

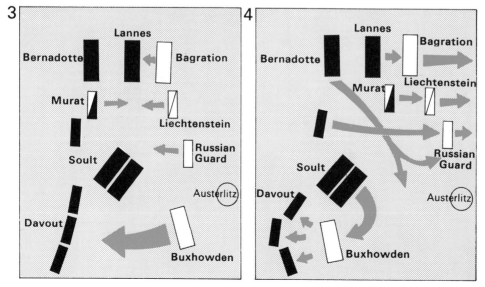

Far left: Buxhowden falls for the deception and marches down from the Pratzen Heights to attack Napoleon's vulnerable right, now supported by Davout. The Allies also advance against the French on the other wing where Bernadotte is coming up to support the French.

Left: Napoleon sends Soult up the Pratzen Heights to split the Austro–Russian army and to attack Buxhowden from the rear. Murat's cavalry drive off the cavalry of Prince Liechtenstein and the Allied right is cut off and forced to withdraw. The penetration of the Austro–Russian army is complete.

were drowned as the French artillery fire smashed the ice over which they were hastening. The majority were captured.

Only Bagration's wing managed to extricate itself from the battle without total catastrophe. The rest of the army was ruthlessly pursued back to Olmutz. There were 37,000 Allied casualties, including 11,000 prisoners; the Allies also lost 180 guns. French casualties totalled about 7000 or 8000. The full import of the victory did not appear until two days later, when the Emperor Francis came to sue for peace and Austria dropped out of the Third Coalition. In the following two years, the French crushed the Prussians at Jena and Auerstedt and then forced the Russians, also, to come to terms. Napoleon reached the height of his fortune, which he maintained until 1812 and the disastrous campaign against Moscow.

Austerlitz demonstrated the success of Napoleon's tactical genius in the clearest manner. He concentrated his widely spread forces at the required point at the moment of battle; he feigned a withdrawal to lure his enemy down from a naturally strong position; he penetrated the enemy line to divide the forces against him and he achieved a successful holding operation to occupy the enemy while he accomplished his main manoeuvre. His tactic of advancing on a wide front, often as great as 90–100 miles (140–160 kilometres), to enable his troops to live adequately off the land also helped to deceive the enemy as to his precise objective and allowed him to move in whatever direction was required, to attack one or other of his opponents before they joined forces. His speed of movement (it was said that Napoleon could march his army twice as fast as any other commander) gave him the necessary control over this wide front and enabled him to concentrate reserves during the build-up to a battle. In effect, by selecting his targets carefully, he managed to bring superior forces to bear against an enemy unprepared for such strength. Austerlitz was a rare instance when his forces were still slightly inferior even after the arrival of Davout and Bernadotte. But Napoleon, as ever, made the best possible use of his available resources.

He also made the best possible use of the local topography. The apparent risk of exposing his weak right flank at Austerlitz was no risk in his mind, because he knew precisely how the enemy would react and how he would take advantage of that reaction to launch Soult's assault. By picking the site of the battle himself and by drawing the Allies into a pre-planned series of movements, he had ensured the success of his attack. It was a master-stroke of initiative and was almost certainly Napoleon's most complete victory.

Napoleon Bonaparte *(1769–1821)*

Born in Corsica, he became a supporter of the radical Revolutionary party in Paris and, at 26, brilliantly commanded the French army in Italy. After his Egyptian campaign, he returned to France and played a leading part in restoring the authority of the Republic. He became First Consul, or virtual dictator, and proclaimed himself Emperor in December 1804. His campaigns against Austria, Prussia and the Russian armies between 1805 and 1812 were the military highlights of his career but his Russian campaign ended in disaster, just as Hitler's was to do more than a century later. He was forced to abdicate in 1814 and was exiled to Elba. He returned in March 1815, for the 'Hundred Days' and, after victories at Ligny and Quatre Bras, was defeated at Waterloo, on June 18. He was captured and sent to St Helena. A master of tactics on the field and of speed and co-ordination between battles, Napoleon was able to merge manoeuvre and attack into one concerted movement. His imitators failed to emulate his success, and the marshals who assumed increasing responsibility for directing his battles, while he concentrated on political strategy, did not possess his flair.

Napoleon's tactic of feigned withdrawal followed by penetration had been used 3000 years before by the Hittites, when they lured Ramesses II and his Egyptians forward into a trap and then cut through their over-extended line by a surprise attack. But in this case Ramesses brilliantly retrieved the situation by personal valour, a determined counter-attack against the enemy's weakened wing and the fortuitous arrival of a reserve force which surprised the Hittites, who were busily looting the Egyptian camp.

The mummified head of the pharaoh Ramesses II.

Kadesh is one of the first battles in history of which we have any detailed knowledge. It was fought between the Egyptians and the Hittites around the city of Kadesh on the River Orontes, in Syria, at the beginning of the 13th Century BC. Nearly three centuries earlier, the Egyptians had ousted the dominating Hyksos from their hold on Upper Egypt and the pharaohs of the New Kingdom had founded a period of wealth and expansion. In the middle of the 14th Century, a new threat arose from the Semitic tribe of the Hittites, who made the city of Kadesh their southern stronghold on the border of Egypt's northern territory. When Ramesses II came to the throne as a young man at the turn of the century, he resolved to push back the Hittites and to re-establish a strong Egyptian presence in the area. He saw Kadesh as the key to Egypt's influence in the north.

Ramesses collected allies and mercenaries as he advanced along the Mediterranean coast, expanding his army to about 20,000—a large force for those early days. But he was feeling his way through unfriendly country and his progress was slow and cautious. It was also loudly advertised. The Hittite king, Metella, had plenty of time in which to prepare a comparable force. His empire was extensive and he could call on a large number of vassal kings to come to his assistance. There were, also, many old enemies of Egypt happy to seize the chance to limit the spread of Ramesses' ambitions. One of the most powerful of Metella's allies was the Prince of Aleppo, who later in the battle suffered considerable indignity.

Ramesses' army consisted of chariots and infantry. There was no cavalry in the Egyptian army of the time. The infantry were armed with swords and spears and carried shields; some also had axes. There were bowmen among the infantry, using bronze-headed arrows and protected by helmets and light coats of mail. Bows were expensive to produce but had already proved to be a decisive

■ Egyptians and Reserves
□ Hittites and Allies
OOOO chariots

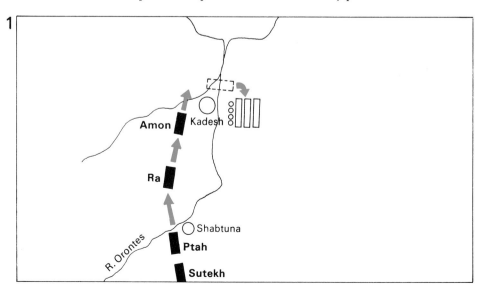

The Egyptians cross the ford at Shabtuna and advance towards Kadesh, with Ramesses and the division of Amon in the lead. As they march round the west of the city, the Hittites, who have been hiding immediately behind the city, move round the eastern side, keeping Kadesh between themselves and the Egyptians.

Model soldiers from an Egyptian tomb. Their lances are tipped with bronze and each shield is painted with a different design, so that every man could recognize his own equipment.

factor in warfare. Charioteers carried bows or javelins and usually attacked *en masse* in close formation. The chariots themselves were light, two-wheeled vehicles, drawn by two horses. The Hittites and their allies were similarly armed and relied heavily on their chariot force; they generally had three men to a chariot—driver, shield-bearer and spearman or bowman.

Ramesses turned away from the coast and marched inland into the valley of the Orontes at the end of May. As he neared Kadesh, he divided his army into four divisions, Amon, Ra, Ptah, and Sutekh, which advanced in order with considerable distance between them. Ramesses and his bodyguard led the army, at the head of Amon. He moved well ahead of the other divisions, with Amon and his bodyguard, when he was within a day's march of Kadesh, and crossed the Orontes at the ford of Shabtuna. Two spies, who claimed that they were deserters from Metella's army, met him at Shabtuna and assured him that Metella was far to the north of the city. Ramesses believed them and pressed forward confidently to lay siege to the city before the Hittites returned.

These spies had, in fact, been sent by Metella to lure Ramesses into his trap. The entire Hittite army was hidden immediately behind Kadesh, to the north, awaiting the unsuspecting Egyptians. As Ramesses boldly advanced towards the western side of Kadesh, the Hittites moved secretly round to the eastern side of the city, crossing over the river and carefully keeping the city between their army and the Egyptian vanguard (Plan 1). Ramesses and his bodyguard had already split from the main division of Amon in their eagerness to surround the city from the north, when two more spies were captured who revealed, under torture, just how dangerously close the Hittites were. Ramesses sent an urgent message back to Amon to join him quickly, but by then it was too late. Just as the division of Ra came up to the city, the Hittites suddenly appeared around the south-eastern wall, having recrossed the river, and smashed into Ra with their chariots (Plan 2). The survivors fled north, pursued by the Hittite chariots, and ran into the division of Amon, who were caught up in the confusion. They, in turn, broke and joined the flight. Ramesses and his bodyguard alone remained to hold the improvised camp they had established to the north of the city against the overwhelming force of the Hittites. So far, everything had gone Metella's way.

It was Ramesses' personal courage and leadership that saved the day for the Egyptians. The memorials and inscriptions raised by him after the battle went as far as to claim that he held off 2500 Hittite chariots single-handed. The poet Pentaur described Ramesses' agonized complaint that all his captains, charioteers and warriors deserted him and that he alone stood against the attack. In fact, he realized that he and his bodyguard could do little more than stage a holding operation against the Hittite advance from the south, so he switched his energies to the eastern flank of the Hittite attack, along the bank of the Orontes, where their forces seemed weaker and more vulnerable. He counter-attacked so vigorously at this point that the Hittites and their allies were forced back across the river (Plan 3). Many were drowned. Others were hauled out by their comrades on the opposite bank, where Metella himself was holding several thousand infantry in reserve. One of those lucky enough to get safely across the river was the Prince of Aleppo, who was promptly held upside down so that he could spew out the water he had swallowed.

The main body of the Hittites had by then overrun the camp but had luckily been distracted by the loot they found there. Ramesses enjoyed a second stroke of good fortune when a body of mercenary recruits appeared suddenly from the west to join the Egyptians. They appraised the situation at once and swept into the helpless Hittite looters (Plan 3). The dispersed division of Amon and the remains of Ra then reappeared and there followed a long and fierce battle with the main force of Metella's chariots. It was only towards evening that the division of Ptah came up from the south, and the Hittites, caught dangerously between two forces, retired hastily into the double-moated city of Kadesh. Ramesses spent the night upbraiding his officers for having left him alone and, no doubt, boasting of the deed he had performed. He had indeed been lucky but it was solely due to his initiative that he had rallied the Egyptians in the first place and diverted his counter-attack to the Hittites weakest point.

Several records of the battle survive but only one states that there was a second large-scale engagement the following day. (Sutekh had by then caught up with the other divisions.) According to this rosy record, Metella eventually sued for peace and the 'abject prince of the vile Kheta', or 'the vile fallen man of Kheta' as the poet called him, was soundly vanquished. Since the other records are silent on this point, it seems more likely that Ramesses was greatly relieved

The full length mummy of Ramesses II, in a remarkably good state of preservation after more than 3000 years.

A scene from the Battle of Kadesh, from a relief on the walls of the Ramesseum. Ramesses II rides in his light, two-horse chariot against the eastern flank of the Hittite army, driving the enemy into the River Orontes.

to have got off so lightly after his initial setback and probably returned to Egypt with his depleted forces as quickly as possible. In any case, Metella continued to hold Kadesh but his power subsequently declined.

Ramesses II *(Pharaoh from 1304–1237 BC)*

Ramesses ruled Egypt for 67 years. He fought against the Nubians, Lybians, Syrians and Hittites and built many monuments throughout Egypt and Nubia. He completed the great hall of pillars at Karnak; he ordered the construction of his mortuary temple, the Ramesseum; he was responsible for the excavation of the rock temple at Abu Simbel. Scenes from the battle of Kadesh, regarded by Ramesses as his greatest victory, appear in paintings and inscriptions on many of these walls. The battle was fought in the fifth year of his reign. Subsequently he formed a defensive alliance with the Hittite king Hattusili and married his daughter. The energy with which he attempted to restore the scope of the empire diminished in old age and towards the end of his long reign there were many incursions along Egypt's borders.

Near right: The Hittites surprise the division of Ra, which breaks and flees north. The division of Amon becomes caught up in the panic and also flees. Ramesses and his bodyguard are left to hold the improvised camp against the Hittite chariots.

Far right: Ramesses switches his counter-attack to the eastern flank of the Hittite force and drives it across the Orontes. A body of mercenary reserves catch the Hittites by surprise in the act of looting the camp and rout them. With the return of Amon and Ra from the north and the arrival of Ptah from the south, the Hittites withdraw into Kadesh.

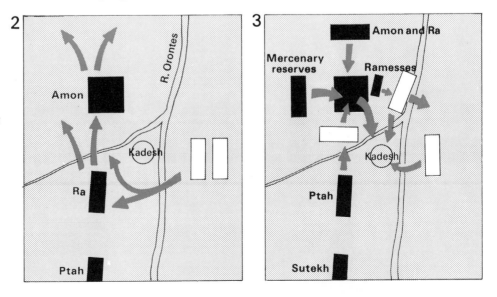

Just as at Kadesh the Hittites had created a situation in which the Egyptians were encouraged to extend their line, making it vulnerable to penetration from the flank, so the Duke of Wellington lured the French, by a defensive withdrawal, into making their own line vulnerable. He turned abruptly to the offensive when their advance guard became separated from their main body. His penetration and flank attack were perfectly timed and he achieved a resounding victory by his tactical control of the battle.

Arthur Wellesley, Duke of Wellington, from the painting by Sir Thomas Lawrence.

Napoleon's imperial ambitions included the conquest of Spain and Portugal. He quickly established his brother Joseph as King of Spain but subsequently encountered much national resistance, supported by the British from their sea-backed bases in Portugal. Control of the seaways after the Battle of Trafalgar, in 1805, enabled the British to provision and pay their troops regularly and therefore maintain a solid defence with inferior numbers. They carefully retained the goodwill of the locals by paying for everything they took, whereas the French lived off the land, took what they wanted and were forced to spread their forces over a wide area.

In 1808, Sir John Moore took command of the British troops in Spain and was killed the following year in the retreat to the coastal city of Corunna, in the north-west corner of the Peninsula. The command was taken over by Wellington, who began five years of patient, steadily successful campaigning against the French in Spain. His tactics were essentially defensive: his aim was to wait for the enemy to make a mistake. With constant supplies from the navy, he could afford to play for time and choose his battleground. When threatened, he retreated behind the formidable defences he had created around Lisbon (the famed Lines of Torres Vedras) and left the enemy to eat the land bare until they were, themselves, forced to withdraw through lack of provisions. By such methods, he slowly edged his way into Spain itself in a series of successful battles and sieges between 1809 and 1812. On July 23, 1812, he transformed the whole campaign and opened the way to Madrid with a well-deserved victory south of the town of Salamanca, on the River Tormes.

Salamanca lies nearly 200 miles (320 kilometres) north-west of Madrid. It has seen its share of human strife, from an invasion by Hannibal in the 3rd Century BC to the bitter clashes of the Civil War in the 1930s. Romans, Goths and Moors ruled it in succession. During the Middle Ages, its University made it one of Spain's most important towns: nearly one-sixth of the population were students in the 16th Century.

Wellington's forces consisted of nearly 30,000 British soldiers, about 18,000 Portuguese and a handful of Spaniards, to bring his total up to nearly 50,000. The French commander, Marshall Marmont, had only a few thousand men less but was about to be joined by another 10,000 soldiers under King Joseph himself. Wellington was naturally anxious to bring the French to battle before the reinforcements arrived. Even so, he preferred to wait for the right moment, a patience which inspired many of his critics to condemn him for timidity. Meanwhile, Marmont continued in his efforts to turn Wellinton's right flank and to cut him off from his supply lines from Ciudad Rodrigo, near the Portuguese border.

The eve of the battle found Wellington's army positioned mostly to the south and slightly east of Salamanca, facing east (Plan 1). His left flank was on the River Tormes and his right flank held the small mound known as the Lesser Arapile. His right flank was also the advance guard of his army as he steadily made his tactical withdrawal to Ciudad Rodrigo. One division, the Third, under Pakenham, together with some Portuguese cavalry, remained on the

Right: A montage caricature of the Duke of Wellington. On the flag over his forehead are printed the names of three of his most famous victories, including that of Salamanca.

north bank of the Tormes. The 1st, 5th, 6th, 7th and Light Divisions were in the centre. The 4th Division held the Lesser Arapile. Their total front was about three miles (5 kilometres). The French were grouped about the southern flank of the British army. Their forces stretched from the village of Calvariza de Ariba in a curve that threatened to engulf the 4th Division. In establishing his position and collecting his forces, Marmont also seized the slightly higher mound, known as the Greater Arapile, after the British had neglected to race for it quickly enough. Marmont's aim was to reach the Ciudad Rodrigo road before Wellington.

Sensing that this must be his intention, Wellington ordered a complete change of front, an astonishing manoeuvre that at once gave him the initiative and created the opportunity for which he had been so patiently waiting (Plan 2). He ordered Pakenham to march through Salamanca and head south, making for the cover of a wood near the village of Aldea Tejada. Pakenham and the 3rd Division then held the right wing of the British army and became the advance guard; they were nearer to the Ciudad Rodrigo road than the French advance guard. The British 5th, 6th, 7th Divisions, together with the majority of the Portuguese and Spanish troops and most of the heavy cavalry, moved into a position between Aldea Tejada and the Lesser Arapile, facing south, while the 4th Division continued to hold the Lesser Arapile, and the 1st and Light Divisions held the left wing, now the rearguard, facing east. A small force of cavalry guarded their extreme left flank.

This manoeuvre was not necessarily a prelude to battle. Wellington was still determined to wait for the right moment. It did, however, put him once again ahead of the French on his withdrawal to Ciudad Rodrigo. Keeping to this plan, he ordered the baggage to set off along the Rodrigo road. The sight of the dust clouds raised by the wagons and carts convinced Marmont that the British were in full retreat. He might be forgiven for this misconception because he could only see the rearguard of the British army, the 1st and Light Divisions and the 4th Division on the Lesser Arapile. The main force of the British was concealed from view behind the low ridge running west of the Lesser Arapile. It seemed to Marmont that he had only to advance quickly enough and he would be able to cut off the British rearguard and achieve a notable victory. Wellington's apparent retreat was wholly in line with his defensive behaviour over the previous few weeks and months: Marmont had already been psychologically softened up for Wellington's deceptive tactics.

At about two o'clock, Marmont ordered three divisions to go ahead of his main force and sweep across the front of the British rearguard. The division

■ British and Allies
◣ cavalry
▢ French

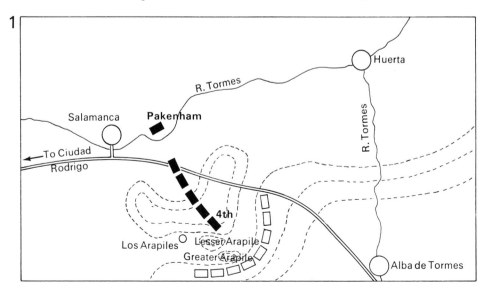

Wellington's army lies stretched between the River Tormes and the Lesser Arapile, facing east. Only Pakenham's 3rd Division lies north of the river. Marmont threatens to round the southern flank of the army and cut it off from Ciudad Rodrigo.

Wellington's cavalry charge home against the French at the Battle of Salamanca. The French waited to pour in a withering fire at point-blank range but could not resist the attack.

commanded by Thomières led, followed by those of Maucune and Brennier. The division of Bonnet continued to hold the Greater Arapile, backed up by Clausel and Sarrut. Two more divisions, under Ferey and Foy, remained on the right flank, facing the British 1st and Light Divisions. As they hastened forward, it was inevitable that the divisions of Thomières and Maucune should become separated from the main force. This was the moment for which Wellington had been waiting. The French divisions were no longer close enough to support each other if attacked.

His staff were having a late meal in the farmhouse of the village of Los

Wellington's dramatic change of front to bring his army parallel with the French. Pakenham hastens through Salamanca to head off Thomières's Division, which is leading the French army with all speed westwards.

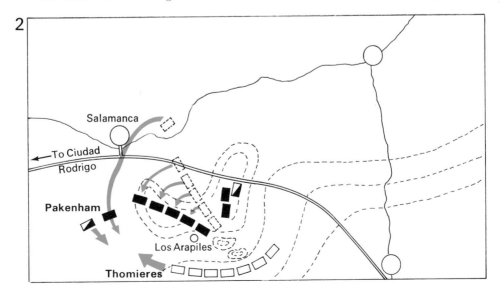

Arapiles, a little to the west of the Lesser Arapile, when Wellington appeared, looking tense and excited. He was offered a leg of chicken to eat in his fingers but his attention was on the southern ridge along which the French were marching. When he saw the gap opening sufficiently between the French divisions, he flung the leg of chicken away, called to his orderlies and galloped off at once. He ordered Pakenham's 3rd Division to attack the head of the French column, while a Portuguese force under Pack kept the French on the Greater Arapile occupied. He then prepared to strike with his main force at the divisions strung out between these two points, with the aim of cutting them off from each other (Plan 3).

Pakenham struck first at Thomières division. Advancing in two lines and holding their fire until the last moment, the British survived a volley from the French advance guard and then charged and quickly routed them. The French were completely taken by surprise and fled back to what they believed would be the support of Maucune's division behind them. But by then Maucune had his own problems. The 5th Division and the whole of the 4th Division, less one brigade, formed the first line of attack on Maucune and Brennier; they were backed by the 6th and 7th Divisions. The British reached the crest of the slope against moderate opposition and then faced the main French squares, which waited for them, with unnerving quiet, to approach. Both sides fired almost simultaneously and then the British charged. The squares broke almost at once and turned in confusion to retreat, just as the fugitives from Thomières's division arrived with the 3rd Division in eager pursuit. At that moment, Le Marchant's heavy cavalry were sent in at a thunderous gallop to complete the rout of the left wing of the French force.

There was a dangerous moment when Clausel's division threatened to attack the exposed left of the 4th Division, after Pack had failed to take the Greater Arapile, but Wellington made timely use of his reserves, and the 6th Division advanced to turn the attackers and force them to join the general retreat. Marmont was wounded and Clausel took command of the already beaten French army. The British divisions had driven through the French advance and centre and were now threatening to attack the remaining French in their flank.

Believing that a Spanish garrison was holding the main bridge and castle on the Tormes, east of Salamanca, at Alba de Tormes, Wellington hastened towards the secondary ford at Huerta, imagining that the French would try to cross there. The British continued the pursuit until midnight but found nothing. The Spaniards had in fact deserted their post, and the French had,

An officer of the 5th, or Princess Charlotte of Wales's, Dragoon Guards, who fought at Salamanca. (The Parker Gallery, London)

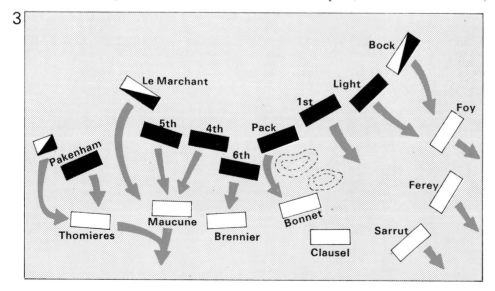

3

Pakenham strikes at Thomières's Division, at the head of the French column, while the main body of Wellington's army launches its attack against the strung-out French divisions in the centre. The fugitives from Thomières's Division join those from Mancune's.

French prisoners being marched into the town of Salamanca after the battle. (The Parker Gallery, London)

after all, been able to cross safely at Alba de Tormes. Bock's dragoons went in pursuit the next day and caught up with Foy's division. Contrary to military expectation, the dragoons successfully rode down and broke the squares of the French infantry, to add a finishing touch to Wellington's victory. Total losses of killed and wounded in the main battle were about 6000 on the British side, about 15,000 on the French side.

Salamanca gave Wellington the initiative in the Peninsula campaign. It was ample reward for his patience. It was also a remarkable exhibition of his ability to exploit the mistakes of his opponent and to change rapidly from a defensive role to an offensive. By his steady withdrawal and his constant watchfulness, he created the circumstances in which he could fight the battle on his own terms, just as Napoleon had dictated the manner in which Austerlitz was fought seven years earlier. His cautious defensive approach was reminiscent of Alexander's preparations before Gaugamela and those of Belisarius before Daras and he seized the right moment to attack as surely as both these commanders.

Wellington also made the best use of the soldiers under his command. His 'thin red line' owed much to his predecessor, Sir John Moore, who had adopted the use of a reduced two-line rank from the Americans during the War of Independence. The custom in the 18th Century had been to fight in three lines, although the third line was relatively ineffective. So long as the infantry were reliably steady, Wellington found that two lines were quite sufficient; they enabled him to use his firepower to the maximum and to extend his line so that it enveloped the flanks of the enemy. Only when he faced an overwhelming cavalry charge did he occasionally add a third or fourth line. The musket in use at the time was accurate to about 87 yards (80 metres) and in good conditions could fire about four rounds a minute with about 15 per cent misfires.

The Duke of Wellington *(1769–1852)*

Arthur Wellesley combined a political and military career. He gained his military reputation as the 'Sepoy General' by a series of victories in India and subsequently became Irish Chief Secretary at the Westminster Parliament. He commanded the British army against the French in the Peninsula and drove the French back across the border after five years of steady campaigning. He was created a duke in 1814 and won his greatest victory the following year at Waterloo. He joined the cabinet three years later and in 1828 became Tory Prime Minister for two, rather unsuccessful, years. As a mark of the nation's gratitude, he was appointed Commander-in-Chief for life in 1842 but his influence from an armchair was less constructive than his influence on the field, where he had shown a masterly appreciation of defensive tactics, a quick eye for the instant opportunity and a sure knowledge of how to get the best out of his men.

Cape St Vincent 1797

The tactic of penetration proved highly successful at sea as well as on land and helped to achieve British naval control of Wellington's vital supply routes for his Peninsula campaign. At Cape St Vincent, Admiral Jervis took advantage of a widening gap in the Spanish line to cut through their fleet. When they threatened to regroup before he had time to turn and attack, it was the quick-thinking and courageous Nelson, only a captain at the time, who transformed the battle into a personal triumph.

A later portrait of Horatio Nelson, who was only a captain at the time of his inspired manoeuvre at the Battle of Cape St Vincent.

Neither the French nor the British had shown any marked supremacy at sea, fighting on opposite sides during the American War of Independence in the 1770s. There had been a notable lack of any large-scale engagements. In the succeeding years, which led up to the French Revolution and Napoleon's wars of conquest, the British greatly strengthened their navy, leaving the French far behind in seapower and seamanship. The British victory at Trafalgar, in 1805, was the culmination of several years of naval successes based on superior tactics and better-trained sailors.

Traditionally, the navy had been used to protect the sea routes for merchant vessels, to guard against invasion of the homeland and to blockade enemy ports. During the Napoleonic wars, the British made great use of their naval supremacy to provision their forces on the mainland of Europe. An active merchant fleet was also a vital factor in British naval supremacy. Had the British not controlled the seaways, Napoleon would have been at an overwhelming advantage but he seems to have disregarded the importance of seapower. The French fleet fought most of the war on the defensive.

The ships themselves had changed little since the days of the Spanish Armada. The British had more than fifty ships of the line at the end of the 18th Century, while the French had rather less than fifty. These three-masted wooden sailing ships weighed anything between 1000 and 2000 tons and were armed with heavy 42-pounder guns; increasingly the lighter and more easily manoeuvrable 32-pounders were used. The majority of ships in the British, French and Spanish fleets had about seventy-four guns. One or two of the British ships had ninety or even 100 guns. Six of the Spanish ships which fought at Cape St Vincent had 112 guns and the largest, the *Santissima Trinidad*, had 130 guns.

The British trained their sailors to the sea, whereas many of the Spanish

◀ British
◁ Spanish

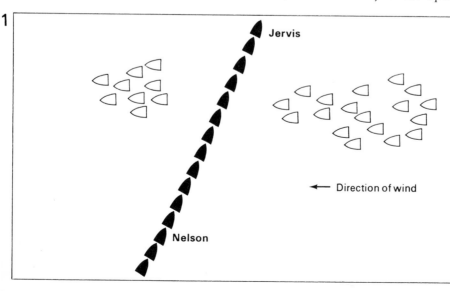

1

Jervis

← Direction of wind

Nelson

Admiral Jervis leads the British fleet between the divided Spanish ships, hoping to cut off the Spanish rear and equalize the odds. Nelson's Captain *lies third from the rear of the British line.*

A typical 74-gun ship-of-the-line, about 1794, very like the majority of the British ships at Cape St Vincent, three years later. Most of the Spanish ships also had 74 guns.

ships were manned by soldiers seconded to the navy. The French, too, used soldiers to fight at sea. Although the 1790s were a period of considerable unrest and incipient mutiny among British sailors because of bad conditions and pay and unnecessarily harsh discipline, the men were inevitably a great deal more skilled in the ways of the sea than either the French or Spanish. Eighteenth-century tactics had in fact gone little further than gun battles. The tactics introduced by the British at the end of the century enabled them to bring their ships to close quarters and to settle the dispute with hand-to-hand fighting.

In 1782, Admiral Rodney defeated a French fleet in the Caribbean, north-

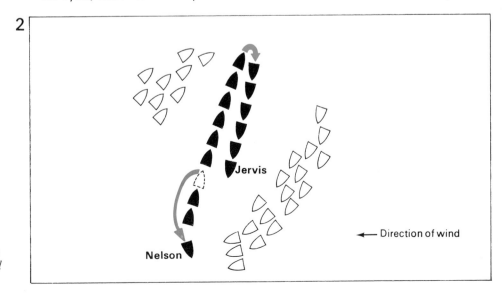

2

Jervis

Nelson

← Direction of wind

The Spaniards attempt to sail behind the British fleet before Jervis can turn to attack. Nelson sees the danger of losing the Spanish ships and breaks line to head them off.

west of the island of Dominica. The Battle of the Saints gave the British domination of the Caribbean seaways. It also saw a successful tactical innovation. Approaching from opposite directions in the traditional 'line ahead' formation, the two fleets opened fire with with broadsides as they began to pass each other. Rodney then turned the ships in the centre of his line to penetrate the gaps between the French vessels which had opened up largely because of poor French seamanship. This enabled Rodney to cut them off from each other and come to close quarters. Despite an hour-long drop in the wind in the middle of the engagement, the French were taken by surprise and defeated.

Another British admiral demonstrated once again how close-combat tactics could win outstanding victories in the Battle of the First of June, 1794. Admiral Howe approached the French in an oblique line ahead and from the windward. This enabled him to cut their line at several points. By sailing through their line and turning behind them, to leeward, he was able to cut off their escape. The subsequent shipboard struggle was completely successful. Admiral Howe had also been largely responsible for developing a naval signalling system that enabled a commander to manoeuvre his fleet in battle and take advantage of a developing situation rather than just to follow a pre-arranged plan.

British fortunes were down, however, three years later. The Spanish had joined the French and the British fleet had been pushed out of the Mediterranean. Napoleon was rapidly gaining control in Europe. In February 1797, the Spanish fleet lay in the port of Cadiz, under the command of Don José de Cordoba. There were twenty-seven ships. Fifteen ships of the British fleet, under Admiral Sir John Jervis, waited outside the port, anxious to draw the Spanish out to sea and come to grips with them, in the hope of clearing the way back into the Mediterranean and dealing a blow to the prestige of France by defeating her ally. Jervis himself was in the 100-gun *Victory*, the same ship in which Nelson sailed at the Battle of Trafalgar. Nelson commanded the seventy-four-gun *Captain*.

The Spanish fleet finally emerged from Cadiz on St Valentine's Day, February 14, 1797. With the wind behind them, the ships made good progress and rapidly split into two groups, the faster ones drawing ahead of the main fleet. This was the result of poor seamanship rather than planning. Jervis was quick to exploit his enemy's weakness and ordered his ships, with the wind to starboard, to cut between the groups (Plan 2) and then to turn and attack the rear group before the advance ships could come to their aid. In this way he could equalize the number of ships on either side while the advance ships were out of touch to leeward.

As the British line passed between the two Spanish groups, each ship poured

Nelson boarding the San Josef *at the Battle of Cape St Vincent. The British were keen to come to close quarters with their opponents.*

a broadside into the enemy. They then had to pass beyond the Spanish ships before they turned about to attack the rear group at close quarters. It was at this moment, before they turned, that the Spanish had an opportunity of passing behind their line and escaping to rejoin their advance group. Nelson was the man who saw this danger, from his position third from the rear of the British line. He decided to disobey the Admiral's orders to maintain a strict line, and to act on his own initiative. Turning sharply to port, he sailed back in the opposite direction to the main British fleet and cut off the leading ships of the Spanish rear (Plan 2).

It was not only a move that demanded quick thinking and a sure appreciation of the tactical situation, it was also remarkably daring. Ploughing into the midst of the Spanish fleet, Nelson found himself engaging several of the largest of them single-handed. They included the vast *Santissima Trinidad*. It was some time before he was joined by other ships of the British line, who had seen his action and realized the advantage of surprise that he had gained from his tactical ingenuity. They also broke line prematurely and a general engagement began in which the British ships rapidly gained the advantage (Plan 3). Four Spanish vessels were captured. The *Santissima Trinidad* itself capitulated and then changed its mind in time to escape before it could be seized.

The news of the victory restored the failing spirits of the British. Jervis was made Earl St Vincent, and Nelson became a Rear-Admiral and was made a Knight of the Bath. His reputation was assured. His independent action had transformed what might have been an inconclusive pursuit and a failed opportunity into a morale-boosting victory.

Horatio Nelson *(1758–1805)*

Nelson joined the navy when he was 12 and had his first command at 21. He served widely on both sides of the Atlantic and came to prominence at the Battle of Cape St Vincent in 1797. In the same year, he lost his right arm in an attempt to capture the port of Santa Cruz, Tenerife. He had been blinded in his right eye three years earlier at the siege of Calvi, in Corsica. Nelson demonstrated his tactical genius at the Battle of the Nile, in 1798, when he sailed inshore of the French fleet to attack them by surprise. Three years later, he ignored his Admiral's signal to break off the battle and defeated the Danes at Copenhagen. His most famous victory was at Trafalgar, when he and Collingwood broke through the French line with their two columns. He himself was fatally shot by a sniper. Not only was Nelson a great naval tactician but also an inspirational leader. He created a heroic naval myth that has endured for more than a century and a half.

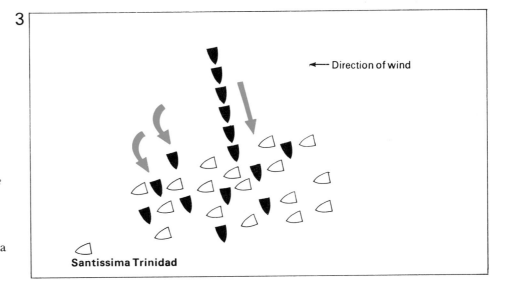

More British ships break line to come to Nelson's aid and Jervis's column has time to make contact with the flank of the Spanish fleet. Four Spanish ships were captured in the mêlée that followed but the Santissima Trinidad *makes good its escape.*

3

◀— Direction of wind

Santissima Trinidad

Battle of France 1940

Hitler's Blitzkrieg attack through the Ardennes in 1940 was one of the most perfectly planned and executed tactical penetrations in the history of warfare. The planner was Erich von Manstein, who recognized the vulnerable gap in the French defences. The most brilliant executor of the plan was the Panzer general Heinz Guderian, whose rapid advance took even Hitler by surprise. The British Expeditionary Force barely escaped at Dunkirk; the French surrendered within six weeks of the first attack.

Hitler prepared for war by a non-aggression pact with the Soviet Union in August 1939. His tanks and air force attacked Poland on September 1 and destroyed the Polish armies in 18 days. Britain and France stuck by their agreement with Poland and declared war on Germany on September 3. There followed the period known as the 'phoney war', a lull between September 1939 and May 1940, at the end of which Hitler's Blitzkrieg was finally turned against the Low Countries and France, and war for the British and French began in earnest.

The Allies made little use of the breathing space. French faith was firmly in the great fortifications of the Maginot Line, which reached north as far as Luxembourg and the Belgian border. The gap at its northern end, along the border of neutral Belgium, was strongly guarded by a large proportion of the French forces as well as the British Expeditionary Force, under Lord Gort, which came over in September 1939. It was along this border that the Allies expected the main German attack to come, just as it had in 1914.

Hitler made better use of the 'lull'. In April 1940 he invaded Denmark and Norway. Meanwhile, he planned his invasion of the Low Countries and France, which he postponed more than twenty times. His initial plan had been to do just what the French commander, Gamelin, expected: to attack through Holland and Belgium, to reach the Channel coast and to prepare for the invasion of England. Army Group B, under Bock, was supposed to carry out the main attack in the north, while Army Group A, under Rundstedt, was to give support a little to the south. Still further south, Army Group C waited behind the Rhine. All ten mechanized Panzer divisions were placed with Army Group B for the northern thrust. None were placed with Army Group A.

The man who saw the weakness of this plan was the Chief of Staff of Army Group A, Erich von Manstein, probably the most brilliant mobile tactician of the war, and the man responsible for the alternative plan that was finally adopted by Hitler. Manstein reasoned that an attack in force from the north would be met by a heavy concentration of Allied armour and infantry. The result could well be a stalemate and a situation of entrenchment similar to the dismal days of the First World War. Such a confrontation would be a total waste of the mobility of the Panzer units that had been so painstakingly developed in the German army. Manstein's plan was to make the main thrust at the weak point in the Allied defences, between the northern end of the Maginot Line and the Allied First Army Group just to its west (Plan 1). At this point, the Belgian Ardennes formed a seemingly dense barrier of forests, which the French believed to be impassable to motorized units. It was the last point from which they would expect an attack. In fact, the British military thinker Liddell-Hart had already suggested that the Ardennes did not provide quite the protection that the French hoped, but it was only the Germans who listened to his advice, just as it was only the Germans who listened to his theories on offensive warfare in preference to defensive warfare. Manstein proposed that seven of the ten armoured divisions be transferred to Army Group A and that Army Group B should concentrate on drawing off and holding the Allied First

Colonel von Manstein, the architect of the Blitzkrieg attack through the Ardennes.

Above: Generaloberst Heinz Guderian, whose rapid advance surprised both sides.

Top: A flight of Ju 87B Stuka aircraft, an integral part of the German Blitzkrieg attack.

Army Group. His plan was regarded with suspicion at first but was eventually put before Hitler and became the basis for the highly successful German Blitzkrieg attack of May 1940.

The Allies played into German hands. Gamelin took no notice of the concentration of forces on the German side of the Ardennes but continued to plan his own left-shouldered thrust against the supposed threat from Belgium. It has often been supposed that the Germans greatly outnumbered and out-armoured the Allies during the Battle of France. This was not so. When the Belgians joined the Allies in May, there were 126 divisions against 136 German divisions. The French alone had more tanks than the Germans—more than 3250 against more than 2500. Their tanks were also more heavily armoured and better armed than the German tanks, although not so fast. The French had fewer anti-tank guns (a little more than half the German number) but these had much greater powers of penetration.

The real reasons for the Allied collapse in 1940 were superior German tactics and command. The Blitzkrieg that had proved so successful in Poland, and which had such devastating results in France and Belgium, was based on the integration of air attack, tanks and infantry, with the emphasis on speed, penetration and concentration of firepower. It relied on surprise shock as much as anything. Air attacks dislocated enemy communications, broke up their depots and, together with artillery, softened up the enemy for the initial

45

breakthrough by the tanks, supported by the infantry. An ever-widening gap was driven through the enemy defences, a protective hedge was formed on either side of the gap and, finally, the tanks and infantry spread out to take the enemy in the flank and rear.

Relying on speed and surprise, the Panzer groups met remarkably little defence in May 1940. The offensive began before dawn on May 10 (Plan 2). It took the Germans only five days to overrun Holland in the north. They advanced into Belgium and, by May 28, the King of the Belgians had surrendered his army. The attack of Bock's Army Group B, with Hoepner and Schmidt's Panzer corps, did its duty according to plan, by pinning down the majority of the Allied forces while Rundstedt's Army Group A made its main attack through the Ardennes.

The spearhead of Rundstedt's attack was von Kleist's Panzer group. This contained Guderian's XIX Panzer Corps, heading for a crossing of the River Meuse at Sedan, and Reinhardt's XLI Panzer Corps heading for a crossing at Monthermé. On their right, Hoth's XV Panzer Corps (which included Rommel's 7th Panzer Division), aimed to cross at Dinant. Densely concentrated and advancing in echelon, this was the greatest tank attack yet undertaken. Although the Belgian Chasseurs Ardennais had prepared mines and obstacles along all the forest routes, they did not wait to defend them as the German tanks advanced. The Ardennes proved to be a relatively minor obstacle.

The leading German tanks reached the Meuse on May 12. The French had barely time to blow the bridges. At Dinant, they did so under the very eyes of the Germans, who hastened across in rubber dinghies. The following day, German motorcyclists found an undamaged weir across the river and infantry went ahead to clear the opposite bank, aided by Luftwaffe attacks, while tanks were ferried across and a pontoon bridge was prepared at the Sedan crossing. Allied air attacks on the pontoon failed to destroy it. On that and the following day, more than thirty tanks were ferried across and, by May 14, Guderian's bridgehead was about 30 miles (50 kilometres) wide and 15 miles (24 kilometres) deep. By the 15th, all three Panzer corps were across the Meuse and in pursuit of the French Ninth Army.

Already surprised by the speed of the advance, German headquarters had tried to put a check on Guderian on May 13, but he won himself a short reprieve in a stormy argument with his immediate superior, Kleist, and immediately put his reprieve to good effect by increasing his progress. He was himself surprised by the success of his attack, which he regarded 'almost as a miracle', but he also recognized the importance of keeping the French on the run before they were

Germans
French and BEF

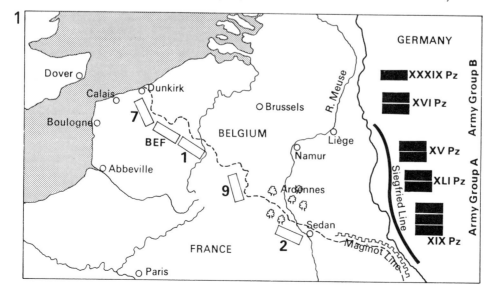

The positions of the German Army Group A and Army Group B before the Battle of France. With Belgium neutral, the main French armies, together with the British Expeditionary Force, lie along the Belgian border between the Ardennes and the coast. Further south, the French put their faith in the Maginot Line.

Above: German photograph of British and French prisoners being marched away from Dunkirk. Not all were lucky enough to escape Guderian's swift tanks.

Top right: Pz Kptw III ausf D tank in the Ardennes forest during the advance.

able to gather their wits and counter-attack. As it was, their own three armoured divisions were wasted through indecision and confusion. The Panzer attack had achieved a psychological blow by striking through the 'impenetrable' Ardennes. Once the Meuse had been crossed, there seemed to be nothing that could stop the Germans. Operation Yellow (later known as Operation Sickle) was already an assured success. On May 15, the French premier Reynaud admitted that 'we have lost the battle'.

Hitler and Rundstedt constantly expected a counter-attack and repeated their threat to stop Guderian advancing so far ahead of the main German army. But Guderian was determined not to rest on his laurels. On May 19, the 2nd Panzer Division reached St Quentin on the road to Abbeville and the coast. The next day, it reached Abbeville itself and cut off the French, British and Belgian armies north of the Somme from the main French forces to the south (Plan 3). With such a long and narrow bridgehead, Guderian himself was in serious danger of being cut off from Rundstedt's army far behind and that was just what Gamelin intended to do when, on May 19, he was replaced by Weygand. The new French commander cancelled the order and planned his own counter-attack. It was almost exactly the same as Gamelin's but the few days' delay saved Guderian and, when the French did attempt to counter, it was

The German Panzer divisions attack on May 10. Army Group B advances through Holland and Belgium, while the Panzers of Army Group A head for their crossings of the Meuse at Dinant, Monthermé and Sedan to break through the forests of the Ardennes and take the French by storm.

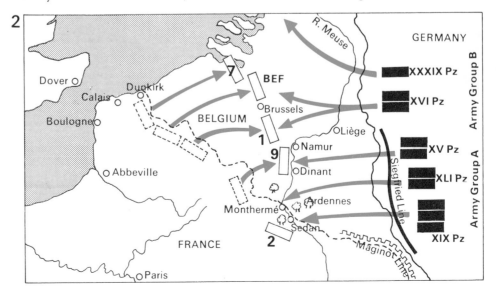

already too late. A French force under De Gaulle made an ineffectual stand at
Laon but a British counter-attack at Arras, on May 21, gave the Germans some
concern. The British very nearly succeeded in cutting off Rommel's division.
Although they failed, their attempt reinforced Hitler's fears about the excessive
speed and vulnerability of the advance.

By May 24, Guderian was still moving rapidly up the coast through
Boulogne and Calais towards Dunkirk. The next day Lord Gort decided to
withdraw the British Expeditionary Force and evacuate to England. His
decision seemed too late. The French howled in protest. Guderian was almost
at Dunkirk. Then Hitler intervened. On May 26, he personally gave the order
for the Panzer divisions to stop advancing for two days. It was time enough to
allow Gort to set up a perimeter defence around Dunkirk and commence the
almost unbelievable evacuation that saved 338,000 British and French soldiers
in nine days. Several reasons have been put forward for Hitler's decision: his

*German artillery on the
Western Front pour
destructive fire on the
Maginot Line.*

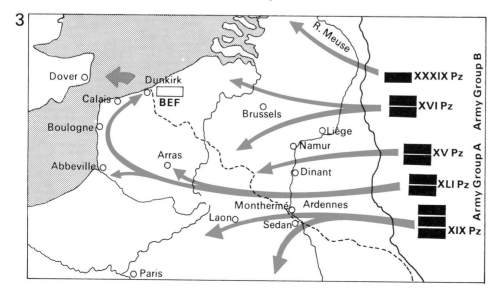

*Despite Allied resistance at
Laon and Arras, German
tanks reach the Channel and
trap the BEF at Dunkirk.
The speed of Guderian's
advance surprised both Hitler
and the Allies.*

alarm at the British attack at Arras (he did not want to put his precious Panzer divisions at risk), Goering's promise that the Luftwaffe could take care of the British at Dunkirk (no one really believed they would escape), or even Hitler's genuine respect for Britain and his belief that their gratitude would enable him to force them to terms more quickly (this was supposition but not without foundation). Whatever the reasons, they gave Britain time to recover from a major defeat.

The second German offensive began on June 5 (Plan 4). The French line was stretched even more thinly and the battle was lost before it began. Paris fell on June 14 and, two days later, Pétain succeeded Reynaud as premier. The same day Kleist's Panzer corps reached Dijon. Four days later, they were in Lyons. Guderian headed for Besançon and the Swiss border, to surround the French forces along the Maginot Line. On June 22, the armistice was signed in the forest of Compiègne in the same railway coach in which the Germans had been forced to sign the armistice in 1918.

The interplay between Guderian's active fulfilment of Manstein's masterplan was reminiscent of the interplay between von Francois and Hoffman at Tannenberg. Manstein's plan of penetration made the best use of German speed and played on the Allies' weakest point (weak largely because they believed it to be strong). Guderian's ability to drive the attack home gave success on the battlefield. Without such determination, the attack might well have been stopped, not so much by the French but by the nervousness of the German High Command.

Erich von Manstein *(1887–1973)*

The plan to attack through the Ardennes was a decisive factor in the quick German victory. It brought Manstein to Hitler's notice but also made him enemies among jealous colleagues. He later commanded the Eleventh Army in the Crimea and planned Operation Winterstorm, intended to relieve von Paulus in Stalingrad. Despite his subsequent removal, he remained the war's most resolute advocate, and the best planner, of mobile tactics.

Heinz Guderian *(1888–1953)*

The major German exponent of tank warfare between the wars, Guderian put his theories to victorious test in Poland and France. He manoeuvred brilliantly on the Russian front but argued with Hitler and was dismissed. Recalled to become Inspector-General of Panzer forces, he also became Chief of General Staff from July 1944 to March 1945.

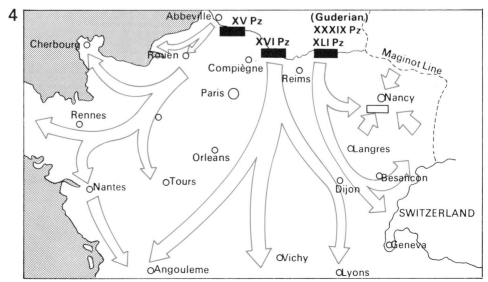

The second German offensive in the Battle of France. It began on June 5. The French signed the armistice at Compiègne on June 22, after Guderian had surrounded their forces along the Maginot Line.

El Alamein 1942

The tables were turned on the Germans, two years after the Battle of France, when Montgomery achieved a victory of penetration against Rommel's Afrika Korps. Employing a feint attack on one flank to distract attention from his main thrust, he was stalled at the first attempt but adapted skilfully to changing circumstances and created a reserve force which broke through the enemy line at a point where it was beginning to weaken. This was the first decisive Allied victory of the war.

Lieutenant-General Bernard Montgomery, commander of the British Eighth Army at the battle of El Alamein.

The war in North Africa between the Allies and the Axis troops of Germany and Italy was characterized by problems of supply and equipment. Each side in turn was compelled to extend his supply lines to a dangerous length as he advanced. Moreover, the relative efficiency of their equipment varied from time to time. After initial victories by Wavell, in 1940, against the numerically superior but poorly supplied Italians, the tide turned in favour of the Germans when Rommel arrived in North Africa in February 1941. The 88-mm anti-aircraft guns, which he put to devastating use as anti-tank guns, were greatly superior to the British 6-pounders. The only way in which the British could respond was to use their hold on Tobruk and Malta to try to strangle Rommel's supply line. They achieved this with great success in the autumn of 1941 but, by January 1942, the Germans had recalled U-boats from the Atlantic to guard their Mediterranean convoys and had launched a steady offensive against Malta. Rommel's supplies were once again getting through to him and his formidable advance along the North African coast began in earnest. His objectives were the Suez Canal, the oil-fields of the Middle East and a southern front against the Soviet Union.

In June, Rommel took Tobruk and the British were forced back to a defensive position at El Alamein, on a 30-mile (48 kilometres) front between the Mediterranean, in the north, and the impassable salt marshes of the Qattara Depression, in the south. It was then Rommel's turn to suffer from extended supply lines. Hitler made the fundamental mistake of calling off his massed attack on the island fortress of Malta in favour of concentrating on Rommel's offensive against Tobruk. This meant that Rommel was advancing with the British-held Malta in his rear. By October, he was down to about a week-and-a-half's supply of petrol and ammunition. Such shortages severely limited his ability to advance in strength and manoeuvre at will. He also faced a change of command in the British forces. In August, Winston Churchill and his Chief of General Staff, Brooke, visited Cairo to find out for themselves why the British army appeared to be acting so indecisively. The result of their visit was the replacement of the Commander-in-Chief in the Middle East, Auchinleck, by General Alexander and the appointment of Lieutenant-General Montgomery to command the Eighth Army. Their first choice for the command had been Gott, whose plane had then been shot down on its return to Cairo. Montgomery was their second choice. It was an important decision.

Montgomery's forceful personality was exactly what was needed to restore the failing morale of the Eighth Army and to instil in it a determination to drive the Germans out of North Africa. He quickly made it clear that he had no intention of withdrawing any further: from now on, he would only advance, but he would advance only when he was ready and when he was sure of achieving success. He therefore set about preparing the army for a carefully planned offensive. Shortly after his arrival, he was able to prove his determination when he repulsed an anticipated German attack in the area of the Alam Halfa ridge. This was a last desperate attempt by Rommel to break through and reach Cairo and Alexandria, only about 50–60 miles (80–95 kilometres) further along the

US-built General Sherman tanks moving off towards the battle front before the Eighth Army offensive at El Alamein. They were armed with a 75-mm gun and were capable of 30 mph (48 km/h).

coast. Employing Rommel's own tactics, Montgomery drew the German armour onto his own tanks and then released a powerful anti-tank screen of artillery fire. He did not follow up the subsequent German withdrawal but continued for two months in making his preparations.

Montgomery had the advantage of unlimited supplies of ammunition and fuel. He also had superior strength. The Germans and Italians had a little under 100,000 men and more than 400 tanks. The spearhead of their attack was the two Panzer divisions, the 15th and the 21st, supported by two Italian armoured divisions, the Littorio and Ariete. There were, in addition, seven Italian infantry divisions and one German infantry division, the 90th Light Division. The Eighth Army had almost double the number of men and more than 1000 tanks. There were three armoured divisions (the 1st, 7th and 10th) and nine infantry divisions. The army was formed into three corps: the XXX, under Leese; the X, under Lumsden; and the XIII, under Horrocks (Plan 1). The Allies also had three-to-one overall air superiority, a major factor in the coming battle.

The German defensive lines included two rows of anti-tank and anti-personnel mines laid between the coast and the Quattara Depression. The lines were about two miles (3 kilometres) apart and were interlaced by a series of cross-lines set at a bewildering maze of angles. In amongst the lines and cross-lines, random mines were sown, forming what was known as the 'Devil's Garden'. There were altogether about half a million mines. The entire defence system was a great deal deeper than Montgomery had expected and it stalled his attack for several days.

With no chance of a flank attack on Rommel's army, Montgomery's plan was to breach the Axis defences along two corridors in the north. Simultaneously, he intended to create a realistic diversion in the south to catch the attention of the Axis reserves. Instead of trying to blast the armoured forces of his opponent in his main attack, he decided to establish a breach and then to contain Rommel's armour while the infantry 'crumbled' the Axis defensive positions in a prolonged dogfight that would lead to a break-out behind the enemy lines. It has often been said that the Battle of El Alamein was totally pre-planned and demanded no tactical ingenuity during its unfolding. This was not wholly true. Montgomery had to modify his plan two or three times and did so decisively and to good effect. Even his initial deception did not have quite the impact he had hoped for. He initiated a series of moves aimed at making the enemy believe that his main attack would come from the south. Dummy tanks and vehicles were moved around, a dummy water-pipe was constructed and bogus radio signals were given out. But the Germans were only half-deceived and did not commit a fatal number of their troops in that direction. However, Rommel did return to Germany to recuperate from illness. General Stumme was in command when the battle began on October 23. When he was killed the following day, General Thoma took command. Rommel returned on the evening of October 25.

Operation Lightfoot began just after 9.30 on the evening of October 23 (Plan 2). An Allied artillery barrage opened up on the Axis artillery positions. While Horrocks's XIII Corps breached the first line of mines in the south, using infantry mine-detectors and Scorpion flail-tanks, Leese's XXX Corps made the main breach in the north, spearheaded by the 9th Australian Division and followed by the two armoured divisions of X Corps. The 1st Armoured Division progressed along the northern corridor towards Kidney Ridge and the 10th Armoured Division advanced along the southern corridor towards Miteiriya Ridge. Their first objective was the imaginary 'Oxalic' line. It was intended that the infantry should reach 'Oxalic' overnight and that the armoured divisions should reach the forward 'Pierson' line. From here they would keep Rommel's armour at bay while the infantry got on with their dogfight. But, on the morning of the 24th, armour and infantry had reached much the same

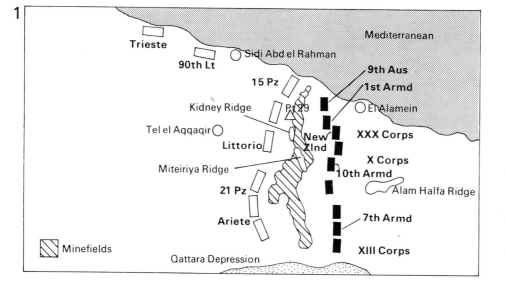

The line-up of the British Eighth Army between the Sea and the Qattara Depression, facing the Germans and Italians behind their minefield defences. The Alam Halfa Ridge, on which the Germans had earlier made an attack and been repulsed, is shown behind the British lines.

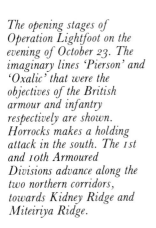

A knocked-out German tank stands as a grim reminder of defeat in the desert.

point. This point was still a little short of the 'Oxalic' line.

The 24th was spent in aerial attacks on the German positions and another attempt along the two corridors in the north. 'Oxalic' was reached along the northern corridor but the southern corridor was held at Miteiriya Ridge. When Leese and Lumsden woke Montgomery on the night of the 24th and urgently gave their opinion that the battle should be broken off because of their failure to break through, Montgomery insisted that they should proceed as planned. His determination to brave a battle of attrition was a vital tactical decision.

Montgomery's 'crumbling' operations began on the 25th. At the same time,

The opening stages of Operation Lightfoot on the evening of October 23. The imaginary lines 'Pierson' and 'Oxalic' that were the objectives of the British armour and infantry respectively are shown. Horrocks makes a holding attack in the south. The 1st and 10th Armoured Divisions advance along the two northern corridors, towards Kidney Ridge and Miteiriya Ridge.

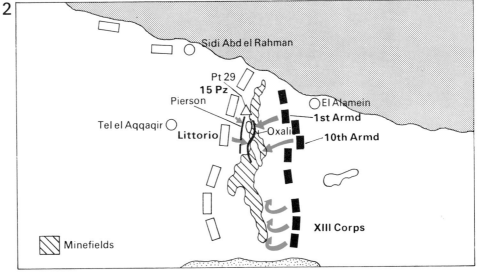

he switched his plan for a simultaneous attack along both corridors in the north to an attack along the northern corridor only. The Australians went forward to seize the dominant Point 29 and to threaten the coastal road, while the 1st Armoured Division continued its attempts to reach Kidney Ridge (Plan 3). That night, the Australians achieved Point 29 and Rommel returned to his command. He at once saw the importance of Point 29 and launched an attack on it. His first advance failed. He then conducted a Blitzkrieg-style attack with aircraft support and with the 21st Panzer Division, brought up from the south, and the 90th Light and Trieste Divisions from the north-west. At the same time, Montgomery was planning to create his own fresh reserve from divisions withdrawn from the front line: the 7th and 10th Armoured Divisions and the New Zealand Division. This was another important tactical move.

Rommel's counter-attack failed but his defence was still strong and the Australian attempts to break through to the coast road were still thwarted. By the 28th/29th, it seemed that after a week of fighting the Allies had got nowhere. Churchill was sending querulous messages demanding to know why nothing was happening. But Montgomery was already planning his riposte in the extreme north, along the coast. Then he made another decisive change of plan. He discovered that there was a build-up of enemy forces in that corner and he switched his attack to a point further south. While the reserve force concentrated for their attack on November 1, the Australians, on the night of October 30/31, made yet a third crumbling attack as a diversionary measure, whereby they eventually reached the coast road.

Operation Supercharge (Plan 4) was spearheaded by the New Zealand Infantry Division and two British infantry brigades, followed by the 9th Armoured Brigade and X Corps with the 1st Armoured Division in the lead. The armour was delayed by traffic confusion behind the lines and then ran into concentrations of the 15th and 21st Panzer Divisions. The only breakthrough was by two armoured car squadrons to the south-west. Rommel recalled Thoma from his attack on Point 29 to hold the salient. On November 2, X Corps continued its western push, while XXX Corps pressed hard against the weakening Trieste and Ariete Divisions. Thoma and Rommel agreed on a withdrawal on November 3 but received a telegram from Hitler that they should continue to fight. It was too late. The Allies broke through on the night of November 3/4. Thoma was captured and Rommel was forced to abandon most of the Italian infantry in his hasty retreat.

Montgomery resolved to continue the controlled nature of his attack and advanced cautiously. The rain of November 6 stopped all hope of pursuit and

South-African light anti-aircraft Bofors gun in action in the western desert. The Eighth Army had aircraft supremacy during the battle of El Alamein.

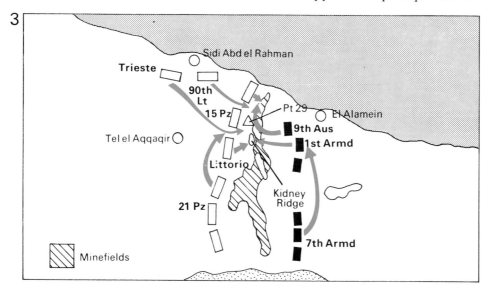

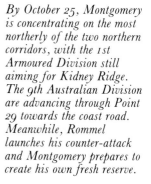

By October 25, Montgomery is concentrating on the most northerly of the two northern corridors, with the 1st Armoured Division still aiming for Kidney Ridge. The 9th Australian Division are advancing through Point 29 towards the coast road. Meanwhile, Rommel launches his counter-attack and Montgomery prepares to create his own fresh reserve.

Rommel began his long retreat to Tunisia. It was not until May 13, 1943, that the Axis forces in Tunisia finally laid down their arms. Montgomery took 30,000 prisoners and more than 350 tanks at El Alamein. The total Axis casualties were a great deal more. The Allies suffered 13,000 casualties, mostly during the first week of attritional fighting. It was a victory for dogged determination and skilful tactical adaptation, as Montgomery probed the enemy for their weak spot and exploited it with his reserve force. In short, it was a victory for clear, logical thinking.

Montgomery of Alamein *(1887–1976)*

Wounded in the First World War, Montgomery gained promotion to Lieutenant-Colonel by the end of the war in a succession of successful staff jobs. After a divisional command at Dunkirk and a subsequent corps command, he took over the Eighth Army in August 1942, raised the morale and efficiency of the troops and won a victory at El Alamein that proved a turning point in the war. He led the army to Sicily and Italy and later planned Operation Overlord, in which he commanded the land forces under Eisenhower. He became Deputy Commander of NATO after the war. Dedicated to efficiency, he studied tactics carefully and was an idiosyncratic soldier who gained the devotion of his men, if not of all his colleagues.

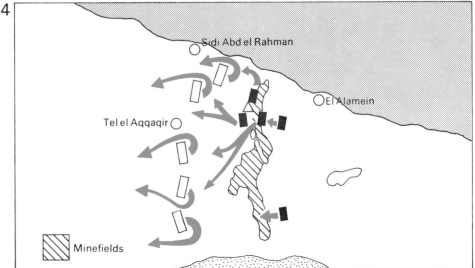

Operation Supercharge breaks through the German and Italian lines on the night of November 3/4. Montgomery finally achieves his penetration of the enemy line after adapting his original plan with great skill to suit the changing circumstances.

We can find a perfect example of the tactics of penetration even in the most recent wars of the 20th Century, although clear-cut manoeuvres often seem rare. Caught off guard by the Egyptian attack in 1973, the Israelis achieved an extraordinary recovery from a defensive position on a double front to exploit the gap between two Egyptian armies. General Sharon's vigorous advance prepared the way for the encirclement of one army and provided a useful bargaining counter in the ensuing cease-fire.

General Sharon, who found the gap in the Egyptian line.

The Arab–Israeli war of 1973 was quite unlike the two previous conflicts of 1956 and 1967. This time it was the Egyptians who attacked first, who caught the Israelis by surprise, who gained the initial success and, despite subsequent set-backs, who eventually achieved their primary political and strategical aims. In view of the technological nature of the conflict and the limited aims of the Egyptians, it looked as if the war was going to be one of attrition (if not outright victory for the Egyptians), but the Israelis found the means to regain the initiative and to transform the battle into one of movement.

Operation Gazelle, conceived before the war and spearheaded by General Sharon under the overall command of General Bar Lev, achieved a major breakthrough on the west bank of the Suez Canal and successfully trapped the Egyptian Third Army in the south. In essence, it was a traditional tactic of penetration at a weak spot in the enemy line, with a flank and rear attack to roll up the Egyptian right wing. The technological sophistication and the immediate tactical demands of new equipment may have been very different to previous battles, but it seemed that the tactics of victory remained basically unchanged.

Under President Sadat, the Egyptians had built up their morale and their equipment to an effectiveness far exceeding its pitch in the Six-Day War of 1967. Their SAM-6 missiles were a formidable defence against the Israeli Phantom interceptors. They were also equipped with an efficient variety of anti-tank missiles, including the RPG-7 rocket launcher with night sights and the portable 'Sagger' missile. The Soviet Union had further provided the 85-mm recoilless anti-tank gun and the 122-mm howitzer, as well as the, as yet, untried Soviet T-62 tank with 115-mm smooth-bore gun. Engineers had carefully practised canal-crossing techniques and methods of breeching Israeli ramparts on the eastern side of the canal. The Egyptians then conducted a series of manoeuvres on the western bank which turned smoothly into a full-scale attack on October 6.

The Israelis must have known about the concentration of force for the manoeuvres and the possibility of attack, but political considerations and the problems associated with dislocating national life by mobilization caused them to hesitate in their preparations for defence. As it was, the thin line of frontier posts along the eastern side of the canal were sparsely manned and were backed by only one armoured division. The garrisons were in fact at prayer, observing the religious festival of Yom Kippur, when the attack caught them by surprise.

The determination and courage of the Egyptian soldiers also took the Israelis by surprise. Later, the Israelis confessed their admiration for the morale of the Egyptians as compared with the attitude of their enemy in previous conflicts. It was said that Egyptian prisoners were closely questioned and asked if they had been given 'pep pills'.

The Israelis had to face an attack from two directions even while they were still trying to mobilize (Plan 1). As the Egyptians crossed the canal and established a bridgehead under cover from their SAM missiles, the Syrians attacked from the north-east, with the assistance of troops from Iraq, Morocco,

Saudi Arabia and Jordan. It seemed that the Arab world had never been so united. The Syrians quickly reached their pre-1967 positions along the top of the Golan Heights but their advance did not endure. By October 8, the Israelis had pulled themselves together and had started to push back the Syrians with the aid of their main strike force of aircraft. Although General Sharon was agitating for an Israeli concentration against the Egyptians before they established their foothold, the Defence Minister, Dayan, and his colleagues considered it more important to stop the Syrians before bringing their full weight to bear in the west. Even so, on October 9, Dayan admitted that he was worried by Egyptian progress.

Israeli troops cross a bridge erected over the Suez Canal in their drive between the two Egyptian armies. Their foothold on Egyptian soil grew rapidly.

The Egyptian Second Army was responsible for the front north of the Great Bitter Lake and crossed to form two salients, one just below El Kantara and one just above Ismailia. It was intended that the Second Army should swing south to join up with the Third Army, which had crossed north of Suez and was responsible for the front south of the Lake (Plan 2). It was the failure of the two armies to link up that gave the Israelis their opportunity to counter-attack and

57

to attain the west bank of the canal. The Israeli defences in the west were commanded initially by Mandler, who was killed. When the war began, Gonen commanded in the south, Sharon in the centre and Adan in the north. Confusion in the first few days of fighting led to the arrival of Bar Lev to oversee Gonen in the south and to take overall command. Israeli command structure was complex and relied heavily on personal relations and individual commitment. It is often difficult to find any one man who was responsible for planning, whereas many examples of individual initiative are found in operation.

The first encounter on the east bank, on October 6, was extremely tough. The

■ Israel
□ Egypt and Syria

1

Caught unprepared, the Israelis have to face attacks on two fronts simultaneously, from the Egyptian Second and Third Armies across the Canal and from the Syrians across the Golan Heights.

Above: Advancing Israeli troops and tanks in the Sinai, not far from El Kantara east of the Suez Canal.

Opposite: Israeli troops in the shade of palm trees on the west side of the Suez Canal, in Egypt, after the announcement of the ceasefire proposal.

Egyptians quickly overran the Israeli garrisons and Mandler's handful of tanks achieved only sporadically successful resistance. Simultaneously the Egyptians sent ahead helicopters to attack and seize the Khatmia, Giddi and Mitla Passes through the mountains of Sinai but they failed to achieve their objectives. Once the Egyptians were firmly established on the west bank, there followed a series of dogfights, with Israeli armour hastened to the front. Adan attempted a counter-attack near El Kantara and tried to turn south against the flank of the Second Army but missed his objective and ran straight into the Egyptian anti-tank units. His 190th brigade was completely destroyed. Because of a misunderstanding, Sharon did not turn to help Adan but, in probing forward to rescue some of the survivors of the Canal garrisons, he discovered the gap north of the Great Bitter Lake.

Not wishing to move their tanks forward from under the protection of the SAM missiles, the Egyptians were hesitant to advance. Their delay enabled the Israelis to secure their position against Syria. By October 13, the Syrians were back behind the line from which they had started on October 6. Subsequently, the Israelis advanced to within 20 miles (32 kilometres) of Damascus but, from October 13, they began to transfer their attention and their airforce to the Sinai front. Better unification of command between the Egyptians and Syrians might have enabled them to co-ordinate their movements to greater effect, but in the initial stages of the war there was no supreme commander.

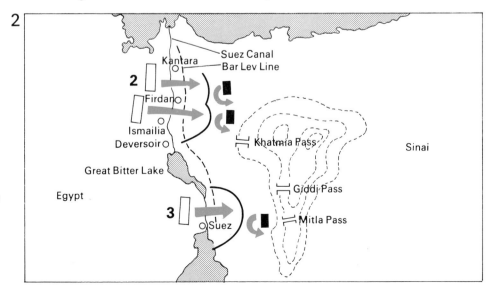

The Egyptian attack on October 6. The Second Army crosses the Canal north of the Great Bitter Lake to form two salients while the Third Army crosses south of the Lake. The weak Israeli defences along the Bar Lev Line are pushed back.

The Syrians had already appealed to the Egyptians to advance but they did not do so until October 14, and then only with circumspection. The Israeli defence had become more solid and the Egyptians did not hope to repeat their easy experience in breaking the Bar Lev line. They progressed steadily and according to plan. In fact the Israelis welcomed their slow advance into Sinai and sought to draw them on, hoping to get behind the Egyptians and cut off their supply lines. As it was, the Egyptian advance ground to a halt and they failed to use either their tanks or their aircraft effectively.

The Israelis took advantage of the inactivity of the Egyptians, to launch Operation Gazelle on October 15 (Plan 3). The crossing site was to be at Deversoir, through the narrow gap between the two Egyptian armies, north of the Great Bitter Lake. Sharon had only been held back by Bar Lev with difficulty for the previous week and, once unleashed, he achieved a crossing with a limited force with which he was able to eliminate several SAM missile sites and thus allow a certain freedom of manoeuvre to Israeli aircraft. There was then a hold-up of about 36 hours as the support troops encountered stiff opposition on the east bank in the area that was known as the Chinese Farm (in fact, a Japanese Experimental Farm). This was strongly defended and saw some of the densest and most bitter fighting of the war.

During that hold-up, with Sharon already active on the west bank, neither Cairo nor the Third Army realized the seriousness of Israel's planned counter-attack. Cairo regarded the crossing as a mere foray that would easily be brushed aside. By the time the Third Army woke to the danger and sent a force north to cut off the supply route on the east bank, the main pontoon bridge was already established across the canal. The Egyptian 25th Armoured Brigade was pinned against the border of the Lake and destroyed by General Adan. The corridor was finally cleared and the defenders of the Chinese Farm were thrown out on October 18. Amidst fierce fighting and with tremendous administrative bustle, more Israeli tanks squeezed across the canal. Sharon reached the outskirts of Ismailia and was impatient to push north, while Adan moved south to trap the Third Army. Adan's force did in fact enter Suez but was beaten back by determined resistance. Even so, the superiority of the Israeli tank crews threatened to ensure that both Egyptian armies east of the canal would, in the course of time, be doomed, with both Sharon and Adan active in their rear.

By then, the Soviet Union and the United States had already started to negotiate a cease-fire. Kosygin had, in fact, been in Cairo to persuade Sadat to agree to a cease-fire on the same day that Sharon achieved his initial bridgehead on the west bank. It was partly an awareness of the impending truce that

Egyptian soldiers imprisoned behind rolls of barbed wire in desert camps on the west side of the Suez Canal.

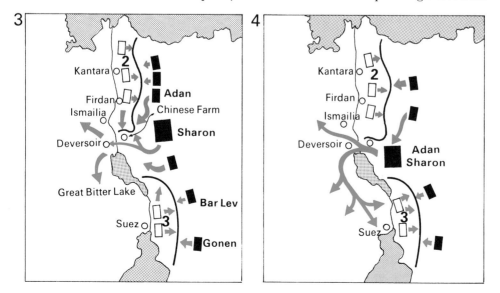

Far left: The Israelis turn to the offensive with Operation Gazelle. While Israeli forces hold the Egyptians in north and south, Sharon finds the gap just north of the Lake and crosses the Canal to Deversoir.

Left: Israeli advances after October 22, the ostensible date of the ceasefire. Sharon and Adan make the most of their advantage and the Egyptian Third Army is surrounded and trapped.

Top right: A formidable Russian-made SAM III missile installation on the West bank of the Suez Canal is captured by Israeli forces.

encouraged the Israelis to push on as fast as they could to gain the maximum ground in the available time. The cease-fire was agreed upon for 6.52 p.m. on Monday, October 22. But the fighting continued for two more days, until Wednesday 24th. Both sides accused each other of breaking the truce and both continued firing, but it was the Israelis who gained all the advantages after the 22nd (Plan 4). They hastened armour across the canal and expanded their bridgehead, pushing south to reach the western side of the Gulf of Suez and thus completely cutting off the Third Army and Suez from all assistance and supplies. The Third Army was surrounded and trapped. Twenty thousand men and 200 tanks gave the Israelis a timely hostage with which to bargain.

Despite the skilful tactics which won them this prize, the Israelis ostensibly lost the cease-fire and Egypt gained what she considered to be a marked victory. The Egyptians had proved that the Israeli forces could be pushed back and that the Arabs could be united. They had also redeemed their pride by regaining a foothold on the east bank of the canal. The restoration of Arab pride was considered vitally important in any attempt to persuade Egypt's neighbours that Israel's continued existence was inevitable.

There were many new lessons to be learnt from the war but there were also some old ones, repeated not for the first time. Israeli flexibility and speed enabled them to switch from the defensive to the offensive with smooth precision: they planned their counter-attack while they were still fighting off two assaults simultaneously. They looked for and found the weak link in the enemy's line and they had the reserve force in readiness to exploit the gap. The direct attack on an unsuspecting part of the Egyptian line proved once again the possibility and the rewards of penetration. It was undoubtedly the spark of Sharon's impatient resolve that kindled the flame of the Israeli advance over the canal.

Ariel Sharon (1928–)

Unorthodox and occasionally irresponsible, Sharon was popular with his troops and had undoubted flair. He commanded a parachute brigade in the 1956 war, where he was caught in an ambush in the Mitla Pass and suffered heavy casualties. He also incurred heavy casualties in the 1967 war when undertaking an all-or-nothing assault. He became GOC Southern Command in 1969 and criticized the Israeli defensive policy as represented by the Bar Lev line. He failed to become Chief of Staff in July 1973 and turned to right-wing politics but was recalled to active service in October. He caused friction among his fellow commanders but represented a strong driving force in the Israeli counter-attack.

More than 50 years before the Yom Kippur war, the Poles, too, had achieved an irresistibly penetrating offensive from a defensive position. Joseph Pilsudski, the Polish commander, sat through the night in his library and planned how to break out of the Soviet net around Warsaw. Like Montgomery at Alamein, he found the key to success in the creation of a new reserve from troops already under fire. His iron will restored morale and speeded the exploitation of the weak link in the Soviet line.

Marshal Pilsudski, a few years after his brilliant counter-attack at Warsaw.

Following the First World War and the Bolshevik Revolution, the workers of many European countries were agitating for socialist reform. Their mood encouraged the advance of the Soviet armies westwards in the course of their ambitious plans for world revolution. It seemed to the Soviets that the 'capitalist and reactionary' state of Poland was all that stood between the Red Army and a vulnerable and not unreceptive western Europe. But Poland had no intention of succumbing to Soviet domination and was keen to regain her eastern border of 1772, which ran just to the west of Smolensk and Kiev. Neither country desired war in 1919, but their ambitions ran in dangerously opposite directions.

It has been said that Poland's stand saved the west from the immediate Soviet threat and changed the course of 20th-Century history. That may well be true. It was also said at the time that the architect of victory was General Weygand (sent by the French premier Millerand), who went with Lord D'Abernon (sent by the English prime minister Lloyd George) to act as adviser to the Polish army. This attribution suited the political opportunism of both Millerand and Lloyd George, who had done everything they could to discourage a battle on the eastern front but who welcomed a victory. The Poles themselves knew that the true victor of Warsaw was their commander, Joseph Pilsudski, who by his own efforts and determination transformed a desperate and bitter retreat into the 'miracle of the Vistula'.

Neither side was in fact ready for war. The Poles were badly equipped and lacked munitions and cavalry but were able to call on considerable resources of manpower, both volunteers and conscripted men. The Red Army, on its own admission, consisted largely of a horde of peasants. It was disorganized and inadequately officered and provisioned but it was better equipped than the Polish army. The Poles made a magnificent haul of Soviet artillery after the

Poland
Soviet Union

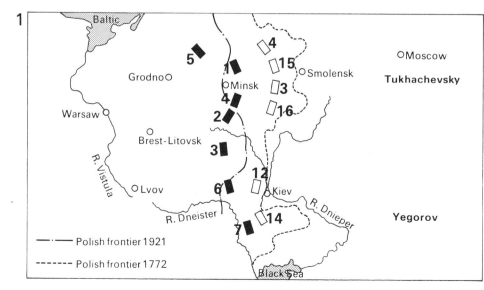

1

Baltic
GrodnoO
OMoscow
5
4
1
15
OMinsk
Smolensk
OSmolensk
Tukhachevsky
Warsaw O
4
3
2
16
Brest-Litovsk
3
O Lvov
6
12
Kiev
R. Vistula
R. Dneister
7
14
R. Dnieper
Yegorov
Black Sea

—·— Polish frontier 1921
------ Polish frontier 1772

The Polish armies confront the Soviet Army of the West, under Tukhachevsky, in the north and the Soviet Army of the South-west under Yegorov, in the south. The front stretches from the Baltic to the Black Sea.

Marshal Pilsudski, commander-in-chief of the Polish Army, discusses plans of the Warsaw campaign with Colonel Kuczera (left) and General Smigly-Rydz.

battle. Initially, the Red Armies outnumbered the Poles by about 200,000 men to about 120,000 men, but with Polish recruitment the numbers evened out for the actual Battle of Warsaw to between 170,000 and 180,000 on either side.

The front stretched from the Black Sea in the south to Warsaw and the Baltic in the north (Plan 1). The Soviet forces were divided into two main army groups: the Army of the West, under General Mikhail Tukhachevsky, with Trotsky as his political officer, and the Army of the South-West, under General Yegorov, with Stalin as his political officer. Tukhachevsky was Pilsudski's main opponent in the north, with, from north to south, the Soviet Fourth, Fifteenth,

Despite an initial offensive, Pilsudski is rapidly driven back both in the north and south. Tukhachevsky heads straight for Warsaw while Yegorov, with Budienny's cavalry, aims for Lvov.

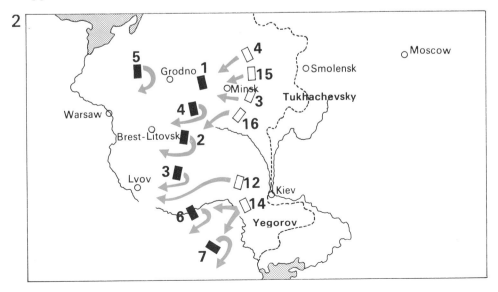

General Jozef Haller, commanding the Polish troops on the Northern Front, inspecting a front-line post on August 13, 1920.

Third and Sixteenth Armies. Yegorov's Twelfth and Fourteenth Armies, together with Budienny's highly effective cavalry, advanced in the south. The two commanders strongly disagreed about strategy and Yegorov played little or no part in the Battle of Warsaw. Whereas Tukhachevsky was determined to break through and to invade Europe, Yegorov was more interested in reaching

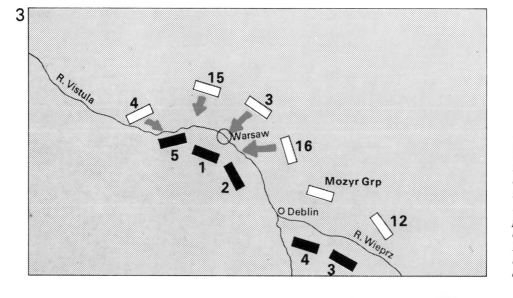

Three Polish armies defend Warsaw itself, as the Soviet Fourth Army threatens to encircle the city from the north and north-west. Meanwhile Pilsudski prepares for his counter-attack with the Fourth Polish Army across the Wieprz to penetrate the centre of the Soviet line.

Lvov and then regrouping to defend Russia. Their division of opinion and force greatly helped the Poles in the forthcoming battle.

On the Polish side, Pilsudski commanded the First, Second and Fourth Armies as well as the newly created Fifth Army under Sikorski in the northern sector and the Sixth, Seventh (Ukrainian) and Third Armies in the southern sector. His chief of staff was Rozwadowski and he was advised by General Weygand. (That at least was the intention; in fact Weygand was ignored almost totally.) Western observers such as Weygand and D'Abernon gave the battle an air of unreality. It was, on the contrary, a frantic struggle between tired and terrified men.

Pilsudski opened an offensive on April 25, 1920 with his right flank and occupied Kiev on May 7. It was the only positive move he managed to make for almost three months. The Soviet armies counter-attacked and pushed the Poles steadily back to the very gates of Warsaw, where they threatened the vital bridgeheads over the Vistula. Tukhachevsky's offensive began on May 15 with an attack by his Fifteenth Army on the Polish left wing at Molodeczno. He was held for a time but the Poles in the south were driven back by Budienny's cavalry. The cossack horsemen advanced relentlessly towards Lvov where they, too, were held. The situation became progressively worse for the Poles from May to August (Plan 2). Tukhachevsky launched all four of his northern armies along the line from Smolensk to Brest-Litovsk. First Vilna fell to him, then Grodno and Slonim during July. Pilsudski could not resist the advance and ordered the withdrawal of his demoralized soldiers. He was driven back from Brest-Litovsk on August 1. The following day, he himself withdrew to Warsaw. Meanwhile Tukhachevsky had decided that Warsaw would be occupied by the Red Army on August 12.

The preliminary manoeuvres were over and the Poles were forced back on their last defences (Plan 3). The final battle was unavoidable but neither side was in any condition for battle. The Poles were psychologically defeated. They were quite openly terrified of the rapid Soviet advance and were convinced that they had already lost. Many of the soldiers wore only tattered clothes, and their shoes were shredded or non-existent. The officers were as demoralized as the men themselves. The politicians, too, saw only the possibility of defeat. They advised the Poles to accede to Soviet terms and surrender while they still could. Pilsudski alone stood firm, although the situation seemed hopeless. In some respects the plight of his opponent was little better.

Tukhachevsky's advance had been so fast and his administration so chaotic that the army had outpaced its supplies. He could not afford to pause and

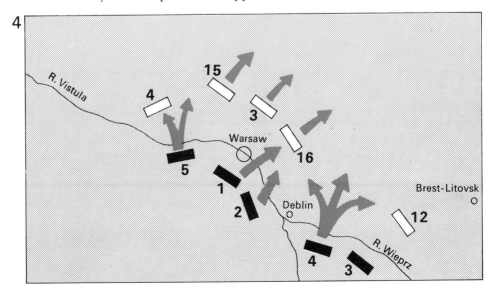

The Polish Fourth Army finds the weak spot in the Soviet line and catches the Soviet Sixteenth Army in the flank. The Polish Fifth, First and Second Armies counter-attack from Warsaw and the Soviet Fourth Army is trapped.

regroup before making his final attack on Warsaw. Moreover, he was convinced that he would be received with open arms by sympathetic socialists once he had broken the Polish army. To this end, he sent ahead civilian propagandists to prepare the Poles for internal revolt. He sought to win the forthcoming battle not only by military strength but by spreading disaffection among the enemy. An anti-Soviet threat from the Crimea confirmed his belief that the sooner he took Warsaw, the better—before his troops became more disorganized than they were already.

The cap badge of the Polish Army.

The two commanders gave their orders for the battle within two days of each other. Pilsudski gave his orders on August 6 for a desperate plan to be carried out on August 17. Tukhachevsky gave his orders on August 8 but his plan was to be carried out on August 14, three days before Pilsudski was ready. The Poles were apparently doomed. The speed of preparations in the week following the initiation of both plans was absolutely vital. Pilsudski admitted afterwards that the battle was a 'brawl' in which whatever plans were made on either side were made without any real idea of the dispositions of the enemy. Attempts on both sides to view enemy troops from the air failed, either because of mist and clouds or enemy fire. Tukhachevsky even came into possession of a copy of Pilsudski's plans, that had been taken from the body of a captured Polish officer, but he regarded them as a hoax, planted to deceive him as to Pilsudski's real intentions. So the two sides blundered into each other.

Tukhachevsky's plan, which should have been implemented first, was simple. Already having the initiative, he resolved to turn the Polish left flank and to attack Warsaw from the north and from the rear. This would also prevent the Poles from continuing their defensive line to Danzig. He requested the assistance of Budienny's cossacks but was refused bluntly by Yegorov after a delay of several days in interpreting the coded message. The Fourteenth, Fifteenth and Third Armies began to move around Warsaw and the Sixteenth Army moved in for the kill from the south-east.

Aware that Tukhachevsky's main force was directed against Warsaw but unsure how far south the Sixteenth Army was positioned, Pilsudski spent the whole night of August 5 in his study in the Belvedere Palace trying to work out how to escape the predicament in which he found himself. Weygand and other colleagues suggested that he should hold the line of the Vistula and counterattack with his own forces in and around Warsaw. This seemed suicidal to the Polish commander. He decided that the First Army should hold Warsaw itself, while the Second Army held the southern sector of the city and the Fifth Army attempted to break out along the River Wkra to the north. This was primarily a holding operation. Pilsudski himself intended to lead the Fourth Army in a daring attack across the River Wieprz between Deblin and Lublin to penetrate what he hoped was the weak centre of the Soviet army, held only by the Mozyr Group (Plan 4). He would then roll up the Sixteenth Army from the south so that it would be pushed back on the Third, Fifteenth and Fourth Armies while the Polish armies in and around Warsaw exploited the confusion to counterattack. The plan necessitated the reorganization of his battle line to create the necessary reserve with which to attack across the Wieprz. The bulk of the troops which he required for his offensive were still in action and beating a retreat. They were utterly exhausted. Others had to be transported long distances across the enemy front. It was a manoeuvre that would have been totally impossible for the disorganized Russians and there seemed little chance of the Poles achieving it by August 17.

Bolshevik standards, captured by the advancing Polish Army in 1920.

As it turned out, it was only Pilsudski's iron will and control of the battle that made it possible. Himself 'menaced by mysteries' and the confusions and fears of the situation, he quelled the scaremongers and prepared for attack. Miraculously, he had repositioned his men by the 12th but was not yet ready to make his thrust. Tukhachevsky himself was not ready by the 14th, his original date for the final assault, although he was steadily building up his offensive in the north and causing consternation among the defenders of Warsaw, who begged Pilsudski to hasten. The Polish commander beat his Soviet opponent to the mark and advanced on the 16th in great agitation. He rode in his car 'looking for the phantom enemy' but, to his amazement, met almost no opposition. He had chosen the perfect gap (Plan 4).

He progressed fast for two days, assisted by civilian peasants with pitchforks and flails. On the 18th, the Soviet Sixteenth Army was in retreat and Pilsudski drove to Warsaw to take command of the counter-attack there. Sikorski had already had disproportionate success with a handful of armour that had penetrated the enemy lines and created a high degree of chaos. Tukhachevsky was 300 miles (480 kilometres) away in Minsk and only heard of the counter-offensive on the 18th. Half his army was on the run by the time he issued his orders, before Pilsudski's noose had begun to tighten. The Fifteenth, Third and Sixteenth Armies slipped away, routed more by fear than fighting. Only the Fourth Army was trapped.

The Poles claimed to have taken 66,000 prisoners as well as a vast amount of ammunition, machine guns and artillery. Soviet casualties on top of that were far greater than the 50,000 Polish casualties in the last two months of the offensive up to August 25. Sikorski followed up the victory with an offensive that reached Pinsk on September 20. Pilsudski destroyed the Soviet Third Army on the same day and occupied Grodno on September 26. He then drove the Soviets back to Minsk and took a further 50,000 prisoners. An armistice was signed on October 10 and, on March 18, 1921, the Treaty of Riga established the eastern frontier which remained until 1939. It was less than the Poles had originally been fighting for but it stopped the Soviet advance and it saved Poland.

Joseph Pilsudski *(1867–1935)*

An ardent nationalist, Pilsudski fought actively to throw off the yoke of Tsarist Russia. He organized an army-in-exile, which he used in the First World War to fight within Poland, under Austrian orders, against the Russians. After the Bolshevik Revolution, he quarrelled with Germany and was imprisoned for a year. In 1919 he became head of the Polish State but resigned after four years. He was regarded with suspicion both by the Soviets and the Western Allies, although he formed a nationalist army supported by the French. His decisive victory against the Soviets at Warsaw was a remarkable tribute to his strong personality and careful planning. He returned to power with a coup d'état *in 1926 and effectively controlled the government of the country until his death in 1935.*

Alexander's outstanding victory against the Persian King Darius employed many of the tactical manoeuvres we have looked at so far. Like Epaminondas at Leuctra, he advanced obliquely to concentrate his attack on Darius's wing. Like Wellington at Salamanca, he penetrated the Persians' over-extended line. He was flexible in offence and defence like the Israelis and, like Montgomery and Pilsudski, he used his reserves with timely effect. His personal leadership was a vital factor, as with all the great commanders.

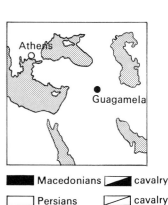

The army with which Alexander the Great conquered Asia Minor and the Persian Empire was formed by his father, Philip II of Macedonia, and it was under his father's command that Alexander won his first major battle at Chaeronea in 338 BC. The Greek city states were defeated and the Corinthian League was formed under Macedonia's patronage. Two years later, Philip was assassinated. Having put down a Greek revolt, Alexander set off on his campaign of conquest. Three powerful motives drove him eastwards. For the Macedonians, it was an economic war in response to the increasing Phoenician trading monopoly in the Mediterranean. For the Greeks, it was a war of revenge for two centuries of Persian dominance. For Alexander, it was a dream of world power.

His greatest strength was his army. The formidable Macedonian phalanx was supplemented by cavalry and light infantry and supported by mobile artillery. Archers, slingers and javelin throwers protected the flanks and acted as tactical hinges. Highly trained light infantry (*hypaspists*) and an aristocratic royal bodyguard of heavy cavalry (Companions) armed with 10-foot (3-metres) lances formed the core of the army. Light cavalry were used for skirmishing and scouting.

Alexander advanced into Asia Minor in 334 BC and won his first great battle of the campaign at the River Granicus. The next year, he defeated the Persians again at Issus, using the oblique order of attack which his father had learned from Epaminondas 40 years before. He marched through Syria, Egypt and Mesopotamia, deep into the heart of the Persian Empire, seeking to bring Darius to battle (Plan 1). Darius finally met him at the end of September, 331 BC, on the plain of Gaugamela, not far from ancient Nineveh, with an army almost five times the size of Alexander's 40,000 infantry and 7000 cavalry. Both sides were confident of victory.

■ Macedonians	◣ cavalry
□ Persians	◩ cavalry
○○○ chariots	🐘 elephants

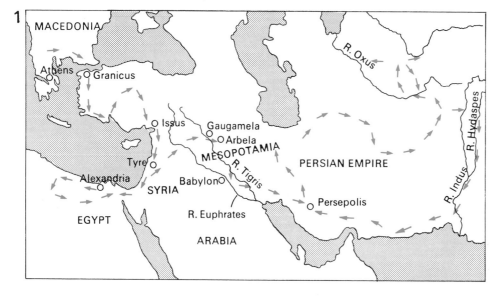

1 MACEDONIA · Athens · Granicus · Issus · Tyre · Alexandria · SYRIA · Babylon · EGYPT · R. Euphrates · ARABIA · Gaugamela · Arbela · MESOPOTAMIA · R. Tigris · PERSIAN EMPIRE · Persepolis · R. Oxus · R. Indus · R. Hydaspes

Alexander's route of conquest from Macedonia through Syria, Egypt, Mesopotamia and the heart of the Persian Empire east to the Indus.

The massed Persian infantry were fronted by Darius's chariots, for whom he had meticulously cleared the plain of rough stones so that they could manoeuvre freely. There were fifty chariots in the centre and on the right and 100 chariots on the left. Darius himself commanded in the centre of the line, with Greek mercenaries as well as Persian and Indian cavalry in support of his infantry. There were Armenian, Cappadocian and Parthian cavalry on his right, under Mazaeus, and Bactrian and Scythian cavalry on his left, under Bessus. In front of the line there were about fifteen elephants (Plan 2).

The Persian line extended well beyond both wings of Alexander's army and threatened to overlap his flanks. Although he meant to strike hard and fast, Alexander was prudent enough to prepare a defensive position that was flexible and could be transformed for an offensive counter-attack. In effect, he created a hollow square. He placed six phalanx battalions in the centre of his line and himself took the right wing with the Companions and hypaspists, in front of whom he put his Macedonian archers and Agrianian javelin throwers to ward off the Persian chariots. To protect the flank of this strong wing, he placed a force of Greek mercenaries and Paeonian cavalry, backed by the rest of the javelin throwers and archers, at an angle so that they could either fall back to repel a flank attack or move forward into the line. On the left wing, commanded by Parmenio, there were Greek and Thessalian cavalry, fronted by Cretan archers, with a flanking guard of Greeks and Thracians. A second phalanx line was set behind the first, in readiness to turn about and repel any attack from the rear, in the event of encirclement. This was Alexander's reserve. Behind it there was the camp, with prisoners and baggage, guarded by Thracian infantry.

Alexander took the initiative and advanced obliquely, intending to draw the Persian chariots towards the rough ground to the side of the battle area and so render them ineffectual. He would then apply maximum pressure on Darius's left wing, hoping to turn it. Darius responded at first by marching his army along the line that Alexander was taking. As they neared the rough ground, he ordered his cavalry forward to encircle Alexander's right wing and stop his forward movement. Successive attacks by the numerically superior Bactrian and Scythian cavalry were met by the Greek mercenaries, the Paeonian cavalry and the Companions, who all struggled to hold their ground. Darius seized the opportunity to throw in his chariots but they proved to be no match for the arrows and javelins of the Macedonians and Agrianians. Horses and riders were shot down. Those who did reach the line of the hypaspists were let through to be dealt with by the second line of infantry (Plan 3).

Bessus's cavalry were finally repulsed and Alexander continued his march to

A portrait of Alexander the Great, struck under Lysimachos of Thrace on a silver tetradrachm at Amphipolis, 288–281 BC. The diademed head is shown with the horns of Zeus Amon. (Courtesy of Spink & Son Ltd, London)

The line-up of the opposing forces before the battle. The Persian wings at first extended well beyond the wings of Alexander's army, which was drawn up ready for instant offence or defence. The Persian elephants played little part in the engagement.

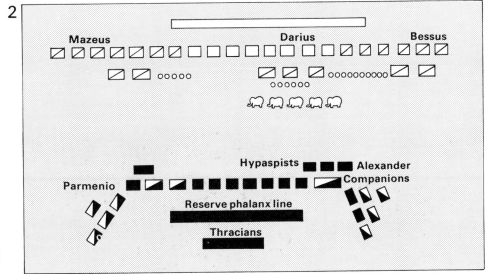

the right, drawing more and more reserves from the Persian left away from their centre until a gap opened up in the Persian line. This was the moment Alexander had been waiting for. He wheeled left, with the Companions, hypaspists and four phalanx battalions, and charged through the gap, aiming for Darius himself. Taken by surprise, the Persian left and centre broke and ran. Alexander was about to pursue Darius when a crisis arose on his own left flank, which had been 'refused' at the rear end of the oblique advance. Parmenio had been attacked by Mazeus's cavalry and was holding them with difficulty with the help of the remaining two front-rank phalanx battalions. In addition a split had opened up between these two battalions and the forward four phalanx battalions. The Indian and Persian cavalry had found the gap and broken

The dead Persian soldier, from the Naples National Museum. His curved scimitar lies by his side. At the most conservative estimate, more than 100 Persians died for every one of Alexander's soldiers at Gaugamela.

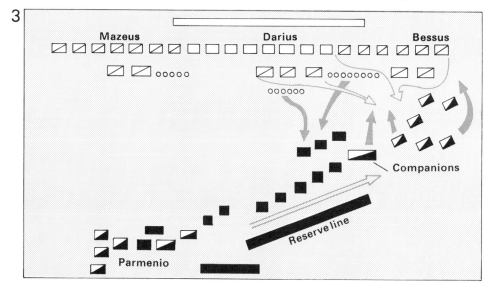

Alexander's oblique advance to his right was countered by the Persian cavalry and chariots of the left. The Persians failed to get round Alexander's wing and the chariots were either stopped by Alexander's archers and javelin throwers or let through the front line and cut down by the reserve infantry.

through. They were aiming for Alexander's camp in the rear (Plan 4).

It was then that the reserve line of phalanx battalions proved their worth. They let the cavalry pass and then turned to attack them in their rear. But this did not help Parmenio, who was in grave danger of being surrounded by more Persian cavalry. He sent an urgent message to Alexander, begging for assistance. Alexander was desperate to capture Darius, and his Companions were keen to follow up their victory in the centre, but he responded at once to Parmenio's message and displayed supreme control over his troops by turning them back to aid his left wing. He was just in time to set on the stubbornly fighting Persian cavalry and to rout them, thus freeing Parmenio and the Thessalians.

Alexander then returned to the pursuit and made a forced march of about 35 miles (56 kilometres) to Arbela (the name often given to the battle). But Darius had already escaped. Alexander marched next to Babylon and Susa, where he seized a large proportion of the Persian treasury, and finally to the Persian capital of Persepolis, where he burnt the palace of Xerxes and proclaimed himself King of Asia. The estimates of the numbers of dead at Gaugamela vary enormously. Some are clearly absurd. The most extreme cites 300,000 Persian dead to 100 Greeks and Macedonians. Others vary between 40,000 and 90,000 Persian dead against 300 and 500 Greek and Macedonian dead. Whatever the figures, it is almost certain that when the Persian army finally broke it was still numerically superior to Alexander's army: Epaminondas had achieved a similar outcome—the mark of a truly great general.

Alexander had brilliantly created his own opportunity by his oblique attack which opened the gap in the Persian line through which he plunged. In so doing, he very nearly created the same opportunity for the Persians. It was his careful defensive planning that so effectively complemented offensive daring.

Alexander the Great (356–323 BC)

Son of Philip II of Macedonia and pupil of Aristotle, Alexander became king in 336 BC. He hated the Persians and possessed an inspired belief in a united world empire and the spreading of Hellenistic culture. His practical genius, together with his tremendous energy and heightened idealism, enabled him to forge the lands he conquered, from Egypt to the Indus, into a cohesive civilization. In action, he combined caution with instant decision and bold manoeuvre. He never lost a battle. Every move was planned with the utmost care. The day before Gaugamela, he went over the ground in person. Abhorring unnecessary violence, he inspired his own men and became a god to those he conquered.

While Alexander breaks through the gap between the Persian left and centre, his own left is in danger of being surrounded by the Persian right. The Persian cavalry finds the gap in the Macedonian line and heads for Alexander's camp. The reserve infantry turn to attack them and Alexander himself leaves his pursuit to come to the rescue of his hard-pressed left.

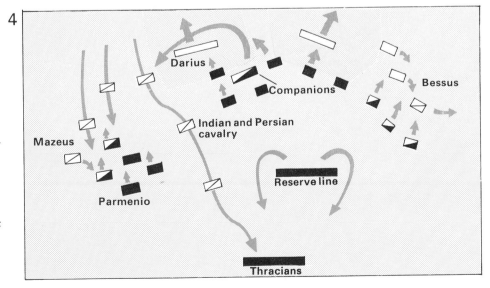

Defensive planning played a major part in the success of the Swedish King Gustavus Adolphus, just as it saved Alexander at Gaugamela. Gustavus's caution paid dividends at Breitenfeld when he was threatened by a double attack on both wings. Superior mobility and firepower, and the use of reserves, enabled him to recover. He drove off the Imperialist left and attacked the exposed flank of their centre. The attack from the flank brought many great victories and was achieved in a variety of ways, as we shall see.

Gustavus Adolphus, who outmanoeuvred the Imperialist commander Tilly at Breitenfeld.

The Thirty Years War, that set the European countries at each other's throats between 1618 and 1648, began as a religious conflict between the Protestant descendants of Lutheranism and the old-style Catholics adhering to the Habsburg Empire. As it grew in intensity and scope, the war became a power struggle among the emergent nations against the old establishment. The Swedish King, Gustavus Adolphus, joined the conflict in 1630 for several reasons. One was that Cardinal Richelieu offered him a great deal of money to champion the Protestant cause against the forces of the Emperor Ferdinand II. Another, was to safeguard Sweden's own position of power. He brought with him the best-drilled, best-equipped, most modern army in the field, together with some radical ideas in tactics that gave him a resounding victory at Breitenfeld against the Imperial commander, Count John Tilly.

The conventional tactical formation of the time was a massed square of infantry pikemen, fifty ranks deep, with four cornerstones of musketeers. This 'Spanish-style' square was as solid as a Macedonian phalanx but a great deal less manoeuvrable. It was to fall before the flexibility of the Swedish formations just as the Macedonians eventually fell before the flexibility of the Roman legions. Gustavus completely changed the ratio of musketeers to pikemen. Previously, there had been twice as many pikemen. Gustavus had twice as many musketeers. He developed a T-shaped formation with the base of the 'T' facing the enemy (Plan 1). The pikemen acted as the spearhead, or stem, of the 'T' and alternate sections of pikemen and musketeers made up the rest of the stem and the arms of the 'T', giving each other mutual support and protection. Several 'T's in a line made a formidable defence against an enemy attack. The musketeers were able to fire at several different angles into the advancing troops. In addition, the infantry were placed in six ranks, instead of fifty, and the musketeers formed into three ranks so that they could fire a simultaneous

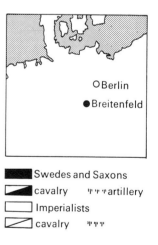

	Swedes and Saxons
◣	cavalry ⵝⵝⵝ artillery
▭	Imperialists
◿	cavalry ⵝⵝⵝ

1

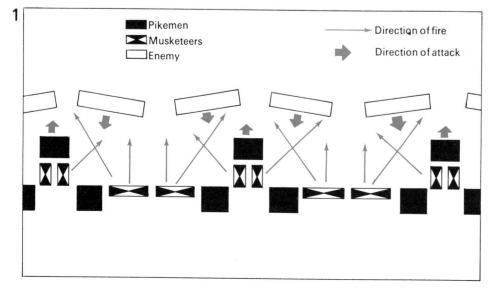

■	Pikemen
◧	Musketeers
▭	Enemy

→ Direction of fire

➡ Direction of attack

The 'T'-shaped formation developed by Gustavus for the integration of pikemen and musketeers. The musketeers were able to cover the pikemen by their fire, while the pikemen could protect the musketeers as they reloaded. An advancing enemy came up against a spearhead of pikemen and a withering cross-fire from the muskets.

The Battle of Breitenfeld. Gustavus sits on his grey horse, consulting with his commanders when to make the decisive move.

volley. The infantry were therefore less vulnerable to enemy fire.

The muskets themselves were greatly improved and lightened. Earlier muskets of 20–30 lb (9–14 kg) had always required a support and a laborious sequence of priming and preparing between each shot. Gustavus halved the weight of the musket, steadily replaced it with the more efficient wheel-lock, and introduced paper cartridges to speed up the rate of fire and equalize the performance of the musketeers, which had till then been, at best, ragged and uncertain. Realizing the enormous importance of firepower, Gustavus also improved his artillery, with the help of his Artillery General, Torstensson. He took advantage of improvements in metallurgy to lighten his artillery pieces and developed a highly effective 4-pounder that could be drawn by three men or one horse. These readily mobile guns were attached to the regiments. With

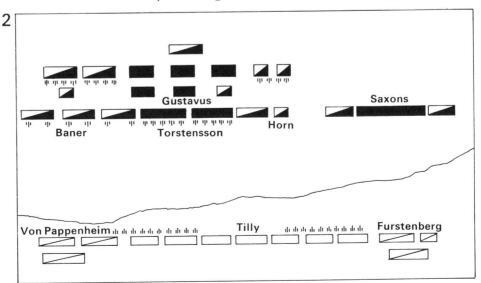

The positions of the opposing armies before Breitenfeld. Gustavus has made careful preparations for defence as well as attack. His weakest point is his left wing, where the Saxons have been placed.

their own charges in wooden cases fixed by wire to the cannon-ball, they could fire faster than a musket.

Gustavus also changed the tactics of his cavalry, which was traditionally used in the manoeuvre known as the 'caracole'. Units of cavalry galloped up to the enemy front line, discharged their pistols and wheeled away to reload. Gustavus considered that wasteful and ineffectual. He trained his musketeers to work together with the cavalry, to provide an initial rain of fire which was immediately followed by a knee-to-knee cavalry charge directly at the enemy with pistol and sabre. This combination of the various arms under his command was one of the secrets of the Swedish King's victories. By this means he provided himself with three important ingredients of success: the power to hit hard, the power to guard against attack and the power of mobility.

Gustavus was a highly capable administrator as well as a military innovator. Among the other reforms that he undertook was the standardization of weapons (to be provided by the State instead of by the individual) and the reorganization of the commissariat so that the army did not have to rely entirely on living off the land. He also instilled a high sense of morale and discipline into his troops, for his new system depended largely on the ability of his men to obey orders instantly. He had already tested his army against the Poles, on the east coast of the Baltic, by the time he came to face Tilly. His eastern Baltic campaigns were on the whole indecisive and were concluded by a peace treaty that left Gustavus much in need of Richelieu's proferred money. But the Swedish army was in excellent training for the campaigns to come.

The immediate confrontation at Breitenfeld took place because Tilly had invaded Saxony to dissuade John George, Elector of Saxony, from joining up with the Swedes. His action had completely the opposite effect. It decided the wavering John George to side with Gustavus and it gave the Swedish king the additional strength he needed to confront the forces of the Catholic League. The battle took place on the gently undulating plain near Breitenfeld, which is now a suburb of Leipzig. It was ideal country for the massed squares of Imperial infantry and for the caracole tactics of the cavalry, led by the impetuous von Pappenheim—or so the Imperialists believed.

Tilly drew up his army on a two-mile (3 kilometres) front, with the infantry squares in the centre and the cavalry on the wings. Von Pappenheim led the cavalry on the left wing and Fürstenberg led the cavalry on the right wing. The Imperialists had about 21,000 infantry and about 12,000 cavalry. They also had nearly thirty guns. The Swedes had about 16,000 infantry, 10,000 cavalry and about fifty guns, but their Saxon allies brought their overall strength up to

A musketeer, similar to those who fought at Breitenfeld, going through his reloading drill, on this and the next page.

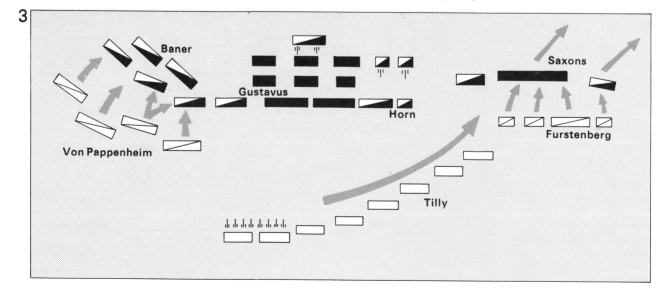

about 40,000, with another twenty guns. The Saxons took the left wing, opposite Fürstenberg. Gustavus drew up his infantry in two lines in the centre, each with a reserve behind it. He placed the majority of his cavalry, under Baner, with accompanying musketeers, on his right wing and the rest of his cavalry, under Gustav Horn, on his left wing, between his centre and the Saxons. The artillery, under Torstensson, was placed in front of the centre (Plan 2).

Tilly missed one good opportunity before the battle had ever begun, a mistake that was repeated by Tallard at Blenheim more than 70 years later. Gustavus had to advance across a small stream. It was not a great obstacle but it presented an excellent opportunity for Tilly to catch the Swedes at an awkward moment. Although his numbers were less than those of the joint Swedish–Saxon army, Tilly's men were confident veterans, smartly turned out and ready for battle. The Swedes were equally confident, but battle weary, and the Saxons were as yet untried. It was noon on September 17 by the time that Gustavus had drawn up his line of battle on the southern side of the stream. The battle opened with a cannonade that lasted for more than two hours. This raised the morale of the Swedes, whose guns fired about three rounds to every one fired by the Imperialists.

Tilly did not appear to be entirely in control of the actions of his cavalry commanders, who were impatient to come to grips with the enemy and to put a stop to the ennervating bombardment. It was probably by sheer chance that both cavalry commanders decided to attack at the same time (Plan 3). Von Pappenheim made a furious charge against Gustavus's right wing and attempted to ride round it to take the Swedes in the flank. He made seven charges in caracole against this wing but proved unequal to the combination of musket fire and cavalry ripostes which met him. At the same time, Gustavus ordered his reserve line of cavalry to move to the right and to face slightly outwards so that they would extend the Swedish line and obstruct encirclement. Pappenheim's attack collapsed.

The battle was taking a very different turn on the Imperialist right, where a general advance by Fürstenberg's cavalry and a large proportion of Tilly's infantry were apparently aimed at the Swedish left wing. The cavalry turned at the last minute and set on the Saxons. In a very short time, the Saxons were routed and Gustav Horn was threatened, and vastly outnumbered, by the main force of the Imperialist army. Tilly had in fact conducted a tactical manoeuvre of some skill, following up Fürstenberg's success against John George with an oblique advance, to bear with his full weight on the now depleted and vulner-

Top of page: A marvellous example of craftsmanship on this Dutch/Flemish octagonal-barrel wheel-lock gun of 1624. Gustavus was instrumental in replacing the matchlock with the more efficient wheel-lock but both would have continued in use simultaneously for some time.

Left: The Imperialists attack on both wings simultaneously. Gustavus counters the attack by their left wing with reserve forces of cavalry but the Imperialist right wing drives the Saxons from the field and threatens to encircle Gustavus's flank.

Right: The Imperialist left is driven off by Baner's cavalry and Gustavus breaks through the gap in the Imperialist line to attack the enemy in the flank and rear to turn the tables on his opponent.

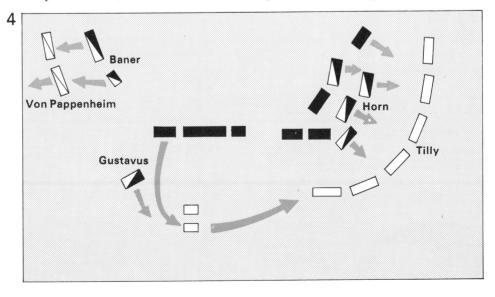

able Swedish wing. It was a manoeuvre worthy of Alexander and Epaminondas and one that was to be repeated with startling success by Frederick the Great. By all rights, it should have won him the battle and he no doubt thought it had. But his infantry squares could not reform their fronts fast enough to take full advantage of the initial success. They were simply too ponderous and unwieldy. As they slowly manoeuvred to prepare to launch their attack against Horn, he rapidly called up reserves from the Swedish second line and turned his own wing to face the threatened flank. He was able to send volley after volley into the midst of the confused Imperialists before they could face their squares in the right direction. In that moment, they lost their initiative but they still greatly outnumbered the Swedish wing.

Gustavus was quick to see his chance. Pappenheim was by then driven from the field and the Swedish right wing was secure. The Swedish King charged up the slope to the low ridge where Tilly's artillery was positioned (Plan 4). He seized their guns and turned them on to the left flank of the Imperialist infantry engaged with Horn. Simultaneously, the Swedish artillery opened up on the Imperialists from in front. Gustavus then pushed home his attack. Taken in front and rear and confronted by the combined tactics of muskets, pike and cavalry, the Imperialists were pressed together. They were doomed, however hard they fought. Tilly was badly wounded but escaped. More than 7000 of his soldiers were killed in the battle and 6000 were taken prisoner. Many more were lost in the follow-up to the battle. The Swedes and Saxons lost about 3000 to 4000 between them, most of whom were killed by cannon fire.

Victory enabled Gustavus to march into central and southern Germany. It also ensured that Germany escaped the Catholic influence of Habsburg Austria. The Protestant cause received a new burst of energy and Gustavus himself became the hero of that cause. The Swedes won another important battle at Lutzen, the following year, but Gustavus was killed. Even so, Sweden continued to play a major part in the Thirty Years War and, five years after Breitenfeld, Johan Baner himself won a brilliant victory at Wittstock, which we have included in this collection. The success of the Swedish army and tactics in the war may be gauged by the efforts of Sweden's opponents to emulate their enemy. Gustavus had founded a new type of warfare, one based on mobility and firepower instead of massed numbers.

It was paradoxical that the tactic employed by Tilly on his right wing, with such apparent success, was turned against his own left wing, with such devastating results. It was unfortunate for him that he was less able to exploit his advantage as quickly as Gustavus exploited his own success. In a similar way, both the Persians and Macedonians had taken advantage of gaps in each other's lines at Gaugamela, but Alexander had forearmed himself with adequate reserves and was quick to turn his enemy's negligence to good account. Once again, victory went to the commander who could maximize his potential and exploit the mistakes of his opponent.

Gustavus Adolphus *(1594–1632)*

One of Sweden's greatest kings and one of the ablest commanders in military history, Gustavus II Adolphus came to the throne when he was only 17. Despite opposition from the nobility in the first years of his reign, he managed to win all ranks of society to his side, from aristocrats to common army conscripts. He was pious, hot-tempered, charming and devoted to duty. He took an intense interest in the study of tactics and strategy and kept in touch with all the latest technological innovations. He reorganized the administration of the State as well as that of the army and laid special emphasis on the importance of firepower and mobility in warfare. Before he entered the Thirty Years War, he had campaigned in Poland, Denmark and Russia. He died leading a cavalry charge in thick mist at Lutzen.

Above: Completion of the musketeer's reloading drill. Considerable dexterity was called for to manage the burning match.

Right: An elaborately decorated powder flask of 1630.

Julius Caesar was a highly original tactician, as well as a commander who inspired the devotion of his legions. He would have won the admiration of Gustavus Adolphus with his imaginative use of a specially created reserve to thwart an attack by Pompey's greatly superior cavalry. Having routed the enemy wing, he took advantage of their surprise to attack their flank and rear. At the same time, he introduced fresh reserves in the centre to complete a victory worthy of Alexander or Napoleon.

The Civil War between Caesar and Pompey was the result of a build-up of rivalries in a Roman state badly in need of a strong, unifying leader. Pompey, Caesar and Crassus had formed the 'First Triumvirate' in 60 BC, an unwritten agreement of mutual support between the three chief men of the time: Pompey, the proven soldier; Caesar, the popular politician; and Crassus, the leading financier. Realizing the importance of an army if he was to fulfil any greater personal ambitions, Caesar at once set about gaining military experience in Gaul and Germany.

He quickly proved himself to be a brilliant commander. Between 58 and 51 BC, Caesar pushed back the German tribes, subjugated the whole of Gaul, suppressed numerous uprisings and made two expeditions to Britain. In the meantime, Crassus was killed, fighting the Parthians. Caesar and Pompey clashed in direct rivalry for supreme power. When the Senate sided with Pompey and demanded Caesar's resignation as provincial governor in Gaul, Caesar refused. He crossed the River Rubicon in January 49 BC, with one legion and marched to Rome. Pompey and many of the Senators fled to Greece.

Caesar went first to Spain to secure his rear and then crossed swiftly to Greece. The decisive encounter with Pompey took place in Thessaly, along the bank of the River Enipeus, north-west of Pharsalus. Caesar established his camp there with a force of approximately 22,000 infantry and 1000 cavalry and waited for Pompey to come and challenge him. With more than double the strength (50,000 infantry and 7000 cavalry plus light auxiliaries), Pompey was in no hurry. He dug in about three miles (5 kilometres) north-west of Caesar, at the other end of the plain.

The disciplined Roman legions, armed with short swords and javelins and protected by their rectangular shields, had achieved victories throughout the Mediterranean world. They had also marched north to the mists of Britain and

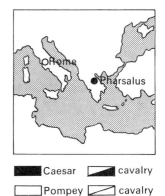

Caesar ▮ cavalry
Pompey ▯ cavalry

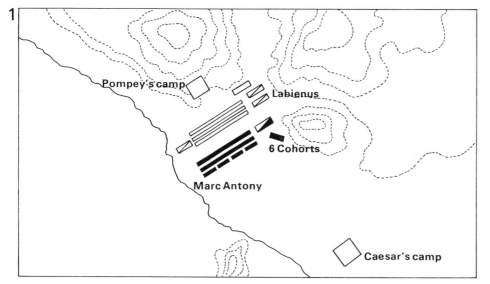

1

Pompey's camp · Labienus · 6 Cohorts · Marc Antony · Caesar's camp

Pompey's conventional line-up, with the majority of his cavalry on the left, is faced by Caesar's subtle variation, necessitated by his numerically inferior force.

the forests of Germany. In their various campaigns, they had often fought against a more numerous, but rarely well-organized foe. The true test of their worth and of the skill of their generals could only be in a contest between the legions themselves. Caesar was vastly outnumbered at Pharsalus and Pompey must have been confident of victory. But possibly he underestimated the character of his opponent. Caesar's personal charisma was largely responsible for the exceptional unity of the soldiers under his command. Their devotion to him enabled him to use them as extensions of his will in his tactical manoeuvres.

It was several days before Pompey appeared willing to face Caesar. Then he came down from his camp on the mountain slope and lined up his legions at right angles to the river, placing Cilician and Spanish infantry on his right wing, with a cavalry force of 600 to guard the river bank. He placed the bulk of his legions in three lines in the centre and the mass of his cavalry, backed by his archers and slingers, on his left flank. He intended that this force, under the command of Labienus, should outflank Caesar's legions and attack his rear. It was a conventional tactic and should theoretically have succeeded in view of the vast numerical superiority of his cavalry (Plan 1).

Caesar made what appeared to Pompey to be the equally conventional response. He placed his infantry opposite Pompey's legions, with their left flank against the river, and set his small cavalry force opposite Labienus on the right. Marc Antony commanded the left wing and Caesar took up his own position opposite Pompey on the right. Before he did so, he made certain careful, less-orthodox preparations, unseen by Pompey. He secretly withdrew six cohorts from his third line of infantry and arranged them in an oblique line, facing slightly outwards, behind his cavalry on the right wing. He explained to them that their part in the coming battle was to be the key to victory. It would depend on them to stop the right flank of the army from being turned by Pompey's cavalry. Caesar then instructed the remainder of the third line not to attack when the first two lines charged but to hold itself in readiness as a second reserve.

When both sides were prepared, Pompey still seemed reluctant to make the first move. He feared that his soldiers would become tired and disorganized in covering the ground between the two armies. Caesar thought that this hesitation was a bad psychological mistake. He strongly believed that his own soldiers' enthusiasm for battle would be greatly enhanced if they felt that they had taken the offensive. He therefore ordered his line to advance to the sound of tubas and a great shout from the legions. When Pompey had still made no move after they had covered about half the distance towards his army, the soldiers

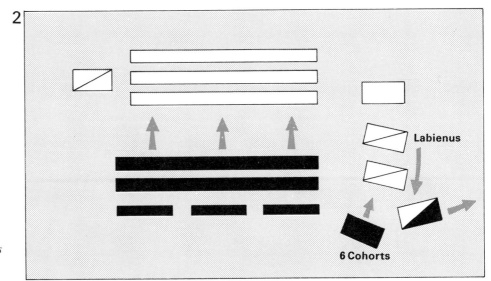

As Caesar's infantry attack, his cavalry are driven off by Labienus who then encounters Caesar's surprise force of infantry lying in wait.

paused for a few moments to recover their breath and then advanced again, shouting their battle cry. They threw their javelins when they were a short distance from Pompey's line and then rushed upon their fellow Romans with their swords.

Pompey correctly determined that this was the moment to launch his cavalry attack, covered by a barrage of missiles from his archers and slingers. Not surprisingly, Labienus quickly swept Caesar's hopelessly outnumbered cavalry from the field. He then turned victoriously on Caesar's flank and was confronted suddenly by the stalwart reserve of the six hitherto unnoticed cohorts (Plan 2). Instead of throwing their javelins in the conventional manner, the resolute cohorts gripped them tightly and ran in among the cavalry, stabbing furiously at horses and men at close quarters. Their attack was so unexpected and so vehement that the cavalry were stopped in their tracks, fell back and were driven off. The six cohorts continued their forward push and forced back the slingers and archers as well. They then attacked Pompey's main infantry line in its flank and rear.

Caesar was quick to pursue this advantage by ordering up the remainder of his third-line reserve. They advanced through the battle-wearied first and second lines and made a decisive break through Pompey's legions, who were beginning to suffer from the surprise of the assault on the flank (Plan 3). The battle was very soon won but Caesar had not yet finished with Pompey, who had hastily withdrawn to his camp when he saw his cavalry beaten and fled again when Caesar approached with his victorious legions, leaving the major part of his army to its fate. Caesar refused to allow his soldiers time to plunder the camp but continued in pursuit of Pompey's now leaderless troops. He finally cut them off from their water supply and forced them to surrender. Fifteen thousand of Pompey's men were said to have been killed and another 20,000 were taken prisoner. Caesar claimed to have lost 200 men and thirty centurions. The prisoners were officially forgiven and formed into two new legions which were then sent to fight in Asia, safely out of the way. Pompey escaped to Egypt, where he was assassinated by the tutor of the boy Ptolemy from whom he sought sanctuary.

Pharsalus was not the end of Caesar's fight to win control over Rome, but it established his superiority and demonstrated his genius for adapting his tactics to the occasion. Apart from the ingenuity he had shown in the tactical deployment of his forces, he had also proved the precept that the general will win who holds the last reserve. His careful preparations had ensured that his final reserve was both fresh and unexpected.

The spoils of victory. A naked soldier places his right foot proudly on a cuirass trophy, from a silver denarius of about 96 BC. (By kind permission of the Trustees of the British Museum)

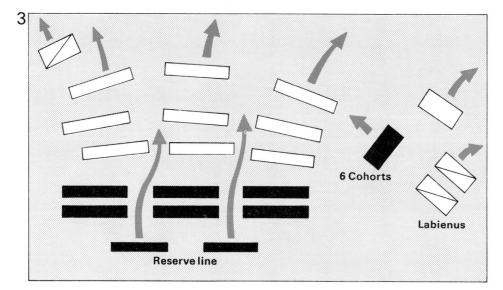

6 Cohorts

Labienus

Reserve line

Caesar's reserve line of infantry pass through the wearied front ranks to renew the attack, scattering Pompey's legions. Meanwhile, Pompey's cavalry has been driven off and the six hardy cohorts on Caesar's right have joined the main battle.

A mounted Roman soldier, without stirrups, reins or saddle. He would usually have reins but his small, round shield was typical of the cavalryman.

Julius Caesar *(100–44 BC)*

Born into a patrician family, Caesar became a politician of the popular party. He was captured by pirates when he was 25 and promised to return and crucify them when he was ransomed, which he did. He joined Pompey and Crassus in the First Triumvirate and began his military career at the age of 40, when he campaigned brilliantly in Gaul, Spain, Egypt, Greece and Asia Minor. The Civil War lasted from 49 to 46 BC and he was then elected dictator for 10 years. In the short time of absolute power that he enjoyed, he reorganized the Roman state but provoked his rivals to murder him on March 15 (the Ides of March), 44 BC. Pharsalus demonstrated Caesar's tactical genius and control of his legions better than any other of his battles. He also accomplished some remarkable sieges, including that of Alesia, when he defeated Vercingetorix from within a double circle of fortifications, one facing out against a relief force and one facing in around Alesia.

Every means of getting around the enemy's flank has been tried over the centuries, before and after Pharsalus. MacArthur tried the hardest way, through dense jungle against the fully alert Japanese in Papua and New Guinea. Holding their centre by a direct attack, his troops edged along the coast to prise the Japanese from their positions. It was only MacArthur's single-minded determination, reminiscent of Pilsudski at Warsaw, that rallied in his men the will to fight in such appalling conditions.

General MacArthur, whose determination drove the American and Australian troops on to their difficult target.

Japan's attack of Pearl Harbor on December 7, 1941, began five months of rapid Japanese expansion throughout the south-west Pacific. Although three American aircraft carriers were luckily at sea when the attack came, the American fleet was temporarily crippled. Simultaneously, the Japanese attacked the Philippines. By March 1942, they had overrun Malaya, Burma and the Dutch East Indies. The Americans withdrew from their last Philippine stronghold, the island of Corregidor, at the beginning of May. The commander of the American and Philippine troops in the Far East, Douglas MacArthur, who was ordered to leave for Australia in March, swore that he would return.

The Americans and Australians retained a precarious foothold only in Papua, where they clung to Port Moresby (Plan 1), whose loss would have given the Japanese the opportunity to launch air attacks directly against Queensland. Determined to win Port Moresby, the Japanese landed forces at Lae, on the north coast of New Guinea, in March 1942. In May, a Japanese fleet heading for Port Moresby was intercepted by an American task force and turned back at the Battle of the Coral Sea. This determined the limit of the Japanese advance. A month later, the Japanese suffered a severe defeat and the loss of four aircraft carriers at the Battle of Midway. From that moment, the Allied forces were once again on the offensive.

As Allied Commander-in-Chief of the South-West Pacific Forces, MacArthur resolved on a strategy of island-hopping, to isolate the strong Japanese bases in the Pacific. The Allied counter-attack started with landings in Guadalcanal at the beginning of August, but the island was not taken until the beginning of February 1943. Meanwhile the Japanese were still trying to seize Port Moresby, and the Allies were equally anxious to establish an airbase on the other side of the peninsula, at Buna, in preparation for their amphibious advance up the northern coast of New Guinea. The struggle for this peninsula

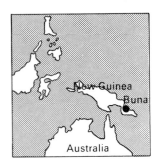

■ Americans and Australians
□ Japanese

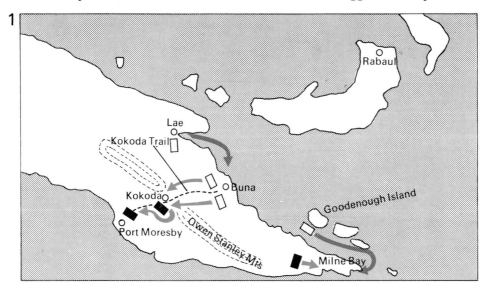

Japanese forces from Lae advance from Buna across the Kokoda Trail and threaten Port Moresby. Simultaneously, they launch an attack at Milne Bay but are repulsed.

Allied artillery firing on the Japanese from Buna beach.

The Allies fight back through Kokoda and the Japanese take up their positions around Buna. MacArthur's three-pronged attack employs Australians and Americans to pin down the Japanese from the front while an American force comes in on the Japanese flank from Milne Bay.

2

Rabaul

Lae

Kokoda Trail

Kokoda

Buna

Goodenough Island

Owen Stanley Mts

Port Moresby

Milne Bay

became a vital factor in the Allied offensive and introduced the Americans and Australians to the rigours and terrors of jungle fighting. It became a severe training ground on which they eventually proved that they could outsmart Japanese tactics on their own ground.

The Japanese clearly set more importance on the protection of Buna and their attack on Port Moresby than the Americans had reckoned they would. Two thousand more men were landed near Buna on July 21, in a further attempt by the Japanese to make a direct attack on Port Moresby across the peninsula. This was not an easy undertaking. Besides having to pass through the dense jungle, they were also confronted by the Owen Stanley Mountains, which ran down the centre of the peninsula. The main track across this range passed through Kokoda, half-way between Buna and Port Moresby. The Kokoda track was known to the Americans and Australians as the Coca Cola Track.

The Japanese took Kokoda on July 29 (Plan 1). By mid-August, with 13,000 men, they were pushing the Australians back towards Port Moresby. They came within 30 miles (48 kilometres) of the port the following month but were halted by problems of supply and by Allied air attacks. A smaller Japanese force was repulsed at Milne Bay (at the end of the peninsula) in late August. There followed a steady advance by the Australians back along the Kokoda Track. They reoccupied Kokoda on November 2. The Japanese then moved back to the northern coastline and established their defences along an 11 mile (18 kilometre) stretch between Gona and Cape Endaiadere, with Buna and Sanananda Point in the centre. The stand that they made there lasted through November, December and into January 1943.

MacArthur himself arrived in Port Moresby on November 6. He planned a three-pronged attack on the Japanese positions, with Australians on the left, Australians and Americans in the centre and the American 32nd Division moving along the coast from Milne Bay on the right (Plan 2). To secure the American flank and to provide a launching point for reinforcements and an attack on the Japanese flank and rear, MacArthur also determined to capture Goodenough Island, just off the coast between Milne Bay and Buna. The Australians were largely repsonsible for the beach-head between Gona and Sanananda; the Americans were responsible between Buna and Cape Endaiadere (Plan 3).

MacArthur hoped to spread the Japanese defences as thinly as possible and, by concentrating the Australians on the left and centre, to enable the Americans to drive hard along the coast to Buna. But the Allies underestimated the

American troops crossing a small bridge near Buna.

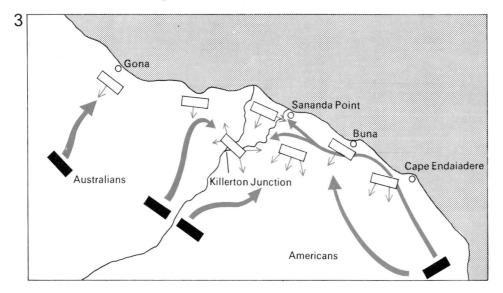

The Australians attack on the left and the Americans on the right. Japanese resistance is fierce but the American flanking attack along the coast eventually forces its way through the defences.

Japanese numbers and the strength of their defences. A further 1000 Japanese were brought in by destroyer on November 17, bringing their total on the bridgehead to about 6500. (The Allies believed there to be only between 1500 and 2000 Japanese opposing them.) They were also well dug in. Their fortifications were carefully hidden, making the best use of bunkers and natural obstacles; they were strongly built and could resist almost everything except for a direct hit from the air.

When the Allies began their advance against the beach-head itself on November 16, they were stopped well short of it. There were reports of panic among the Americans, who appeared shell-shocked by the unexpectedly awful conditions and by the fierce resistance of the Japanese snipers. But it was the jungle more than the Japanese that really frightened them. Unable to force the Japanese positions directly, the Australians and Americans in the centre made several attempts around Killerton's road junction, and another point on the trail known as Huggins' road block, to make wide sweeps round either flank of the Japanese entrenchments and to come at them from the rear. In one incident, ninety men reached a point two miles (3 kilometres) behind the Japanese and crept up through the jungle to within 50 yards (46 metres) of them. Both sides suffered heavy losses in the fight that followed. There were many other similar incidents.

MacArthur took a firm hand on November 30, when he relieved the local commander and replaced him by Lieutenant-General Robert Eichelberger. 'I want you to take Buna or not come back alive,' he said. Eichelberger managed to restore the fighting spirit of the Americans by his personal participation in the attacks, but little progress was made in the centre during December, despite the use of tanks, replacements and air attacks. The flank attack on the right was making better progress, although slowly, and forcing its way around to the east of Buna (Plan 3). MacArthur's tactics were paying off.

Relief troops arrived from Goodenough Island on December 31 and an attack was launched on January 1, 1943. Buna Mission fell on January 2. Nearly 1400 Japanese were found dead there, fifty were taken prisoner and about 200–300 escaped. Sanananda village fell on January 18. This enabled the Americans on the right to join up with the Australians and encircle the remaining Japanese in the Killerton junction area.

It had been a hard slog against formidable odds but MacArthur had achieved his objective through tactical good sense and his own powerful determination. The last pocket of resistance was wiped up on January 21. From a total force of 20,000 the Japanese had lost about 13,000 dead since the previous March. Australian battle casualties since the previous July had been about 5700 in all. American battle casualties had been about 2850 in the same time. The victory had been a costly struggle.

Douglas MacArthur *(1880–1964)*

A veteran of the First World War, MacArthur organized the army of the Philippines in 1935 and retired in 1937. He was recalled in 1941 and appointed commander of all forces in the Philippines but was forced out by the Japanese in March 1942. Later that year, he began his island-hopping return. He became Supreme Commander of the Allied Forces on land in the Pacific and received the Japanese surrender on board USS Missouri in September 1945. Subsequently, he spent five years as Chief of the Occupation Forces in Japan and, in 1950, became head of the United Nations forces in Korea, at the age of 70. He argued with President Truman the following year and was dismissed. His particular skill was amphibious warfare. He combined a strong personality with both tactical and strategical awareness.

In total contrast to MacArthur's experience at Buna, the flanking attack may sometimes occur almost by chance, as at Marathon. Even so, Miltiades, like Julius Caesar and many other great commanders, recognized the importance of seizing the initiative. When the Greeks advanced in the traditional head-on collision with the Persians, their centre fell behind, drawing the Persians on, and their wings were able to attack the Persian flanks in an opportunist manoeuvre that presaged Hannibal's cunning ploy at Cannae.

Miltiades, who persuaded his fellow commanders to take the bold approach against the Persians.

The fastest growing power in Asia Minor at the beginning of the 5th Century BC was undoubtedly that of the Persians. An efficiently run empire, controlled and expanded by a reorganized army, had first been established by Cyrus II, who died in 530 BC. This empire was consolidated by his son-in-law, Darius I. It was Darius who extended the Persian campaigns south into Egypt, east to the Indus River and west, across the Bosphorus, into Europe. In 511 BC, Darius crossed the Danube in vain pursuit of the Scythians.

At this time, Athens was still shrugging off her tyrant rulers. The democratic reforms of Cleisthenes were introduced only a few years before the turn of the century. Greece and the Ionian islands were merely a discordant collection of warring city states already feeling the heavy hand of the spreading Persian empire. New alliances were formed to meet the eastern threat. In 500 BC, Miletus, on the mainland of Asia Minor, together with Athens and Eretrea, marched against the Persian provincial capital of Sardes and burnt it. The Allies were subsequently defeated at Ephesus and Darius sent a punitive expedition whose fleet was destroyed in a storm off Mount Athos. Undeterred and set on revenge, Darius organized another campaign two years later, in 490 BC. It was led by the satraps Datis and Artaphernes and accompanied by the banished tyrant of Athens, Hippias, who was hoping to be reinstated after the Athenians had been defeated.

The two satraps, with an army of 60,000, had been ordered by Darius to enslave the citizens of Eretrea and Athens and to bring them before him in chains. They had little trouble with the Eretreans, aided by treachery from within. The Persians burnt their city and held the Eretreans captive on a neighbouring island to await the arrival of the Athenian prisoners, whom they anticipated taking with equal ease. It was probably Hippias who advised them to land from their fleet in the Bay of Marathon, 22 miles (35 kilometres)

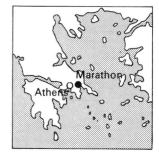

Greeks
Persians
fleet

The Persians stand with their backs to the Bay of Marathon, facing the Athenians and Plataeans. Even when more than half their force had been sent round by sea towards Athens, the remaining Persian force was almost double that of the Greeks.

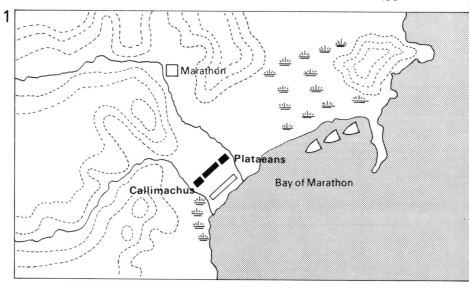

1

Marathon

Plataeans

Callimachus

Bay of Marathon

*Below: The bronze figure of
a Greek hoplite from
Dodona, about 520 BC.*

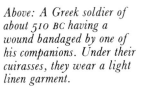

*Above: A Greek soldier of
about 510 BC having a
wound bandaged by one of
his companions. Under their
cuirasses, they wear a light
linen garment.*

north-east of Athens. There, on the level plain, 5–6 miles long (8–10 kilometres) and two miles deep (3 kilometres), with mountains behind and to the west and with a stream and marshy ground to the east, Hippias believed that the Persians would be able to use their cavalry to the best advantage against the numerically inferior Athenians (Plan 1).

The Persian force consisted of a large number of cavalry, archers, missile throwers and light infantry, insufficiently protected by wicker shields, turbans and tunics. The force that confronted the Athenians was in fact only the rearguard of the expedition and consisted of about 20,000 men. Datis had made the mistake of dividing his army and sending a part of it on by sea to attack Athens. On their side, the Athenians had neither cavalry nor archers. Their heavy infantry, or hoplites, were steadfast citizen-soldiers, well-disciplined and well-armed, with short swords and spears that were 21 feet (6.4 metres) long. They were protected by bronze armour in the form of round shields, helmets, breastplates and greaves. The Greek phalanx, eight-men deep, was a formidable weapon of attack, just as the Macedonian phalanx was to prove itself 150

years later. There were about 10,000 Athenians, who were joined by 1000 Plataeans. These people owed Athens a debt for Athenian protection against Plataea's aggressive neighbour, Thebes. Athens had also sent for assistance to Sparta but the Spartans were in the middle of a religious festival and did not turn up until after the main battle was over.

The Athenian command was organized largely by committee. There were ten generals, with the casting vote going to the war chief, or 'polemarch', Callimachus. The most forceful general and the man who was responsible for the positive action that brought success to the Athenians was Miltiades. It was he who persuaded Callimachus to take the bold approach when the generals were split between holding back their army to defend Athens and marching against the Persians to force them to fight before they reached the city. The generals, in pairs, took it in turn to command the army and it was Miltiades who had sole command on the crucial day, his partner having given up his 'share' on this occasion.

With their backs to the sea and their fleet drawn up further along the beach, the Persians were hesitant to make a move. Miltiades ordered the Athenian line to be spread thinly across the valley so that the Persian cavalry could not get round behind the attack from the rear. Callimachus took the right wing and the Plataeans held the left. Both wings were given extra weight at the expense of the centre, under Themistocles and Aristides. (Ten years later, both these generals were to make their own names, the first at Salamis, the second at Plataea.) The armies in fact faced each other for several days before the battle.

The order for the Athenians to take the initiative and attack was given during the afternoon, towards the end of September 490 BC, while the Greeks were still about a mile away from the front line of the massed Persian army. The hoplites broke into a run as they advanced, partly to prevent a cavalry counter-manoeuvre and partly to get in under the rain of missiles that were fired at them. Their disciplined training and fitness enabled them to keep a fairly steady line as they advanced but as they closed with the enemy their more

A Greek hoplite phalanx marches into battle to the sound of music, from a vase painting. These are wearing shin greaves and helmets similar to the bronze figure on the previous page.

Right: The stronger wings of the Greek force advance a little ahead of the centre as they approach the Persian line.

Far right: As the Persians compress their line to bring their weight to bear against the faltering Athenian centre, the Greek wings seize the opportunity to attack the exposed Persian flanks. The Athenian centre holds and the Persians are defeated.

confident wings swept forward and their weakened centre hung back a little, so that the whole line formed a crescent as it met the Persians (Plan 2).

The formation was probably fortuitous, although it would be nice to credit it to the tactical ingenuity of Miltiades. All the same, he knew how to press home his advantage. As the weight of the Persian centre rapidly pushed back the Athenian centre and threatened to break it, the Athenians withdrew further and the Greek wings pressed inward against the flanks of the Asians on the Persian wings (Plan 3). When the critical moment was reached in the centre and it seemed that the Persians must break through, their wings collapsed and the army broke in panic and confusion. Callimachus was killed in the struggle to harass the Persians as they hastily boarded their ships. It was reported that 192 Athenians and about 100 Plataeans fell in the battle, whereas 6400 Persians were killed.

Datis at once set sail for Athens, hoping to join the rest of his force and to reach the city while it was still undefended. He hoped also to take advantage of the subversive elements within the city and to win it through betrayal just as he had won Eretrea. Miltiades anticipated this move. First he sent the famous 'Marathon' runner to Athens, with the news of the victory. Then, with his army, he raced back across the land route and was in time to confront Datis's fleet as it rounded Cape Sounion and arrived before the harbour of Athens. Datis took one look at the triumphant hoplites and withdrew. The Persian campaign was finished, for the time being.

The Athenians were aided by the failure of the Persian cavalry to play any part in the battle. (They were in fact absent when the battle opened but they constituted a permanent threat.) But victory was really due to the superbly disciplined Greek phalanx and the prompt initiative of Miltiades, who knew how to make the most of his resources and his opportunities.

Miltiades *(died c. 488 BC)*

Having been sent by the tyrant of Athens to rule the principality of the Chersonese in about 518 BC, Miltiades gained valuable experience of the Persian army when forced to submit to Darius and join his expedition to Scythia. He plotted to cut off Darius's retreat across the Danube and, after conquering the islands of Lemnos and Imbros on behalf of Athens, he was forced to flee from his principality to avoid Darius's revenge. He incurred the suspicion of many democratic Athenians for his noble connections, but his Persian experience led to his appointment as one of the ten generals at Marathon. He later led a fleet to regain Athenian control of the Aegean but died of a wound in 448 BC.

A silver coin (siglos) showing the Persian King Darius kneeling to fire an arrow. (By kind permission of the Trustees of the British Museum)

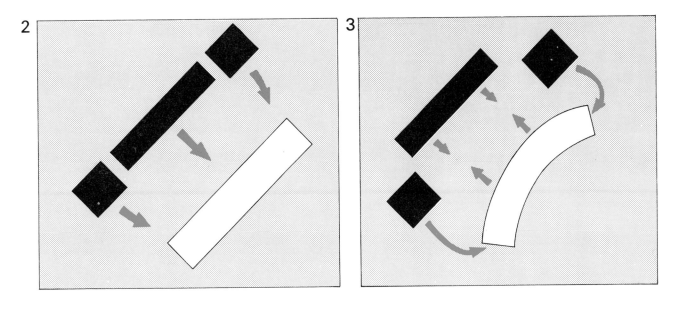

Ten years after Marathon, the Greeks also defeated the Persians at sea. Like Miltiades, the Athenian Themistocles was almost alone among his colleagues in his determination to seize the initiative, but in this case he used a trick to lure the great Persian fleet forward into a narrow channel, where they lost the advantage of numbers. With maximum strength on one wing, Themistocles successfully sailed round the Persian flank, a tactical manoeuvre that proved as effective at sea as it had been on land.

Themistocles, who laid the carefully planned trap for the Persian fleet at Salamis.

When Xerxes succeeded Darius in 485 BC, he determined to invade Greece once again and to crush the city states. The army that he led through Thrace and Macedon and down through Thessaly towards Athens was reputed to be 160,000 strong. It was accompanied by a fleet of more than 1200 warships and 3000 transports. This was to be a conclusive campaign, on which Xerxes was prepared to stake his prestige in the west.

In response to this challenge, a defensive alliance was formed in which Athens and Sparta were the dominant members. Their strength this time lay mainly in their fleet of triremes, which Themistocles, the Athenian leader, had built up in the decade since Marathon. The Greeks hoped to force the Persians into a naval battle that would give them control of the Aegean, deprive Xerxes of his transports and set at risk his lines of communication with his bases back home in Asia Minor.

The Greek triremes had been developed during the last half of the 6th Century. Anything up to 170 rowers, each taking one oar, were arranged in three overlapping rows. The ships were very solid but also highly manoeuvrable. Their tactic was to render the opposition immobile by smashing their oars, then to ram them and send in a boarding party of hoplite marines. On this occasion, the joint fleet of the Allies consisted of 324 triremes and nine penteconters. Athens provided the main contingent of 180 ships under the command of Themistocles. Sparta provided only a handful of ten ships but, as they were the senior partners in the alliance, their commander, Eurybiades, was given overall command of the fleet. In addition there was a land force of about 7000 hoplites and 300 Spartans under the leadership of the Spartan king Leonidas.

Just as at Marathon Miltiades had realized the need to bring the Persians to battle before they neared Athens, so Themistocles, as the brain behind the

- ◼ Greeks
- ◻ Persians

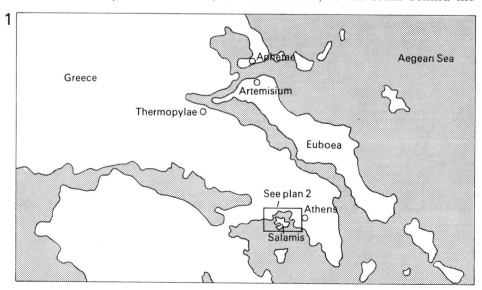

1

Themistocles plans to hold the Persian army at Thermopylae and force the Persians to fight a naval battle in the channel between Euboea and the mainland, where the more highly manoeuvrable Greek ships would have the advantage.

Allied plans, was anxious to precipitate a sea battle before the Persian land forces came too far south. Leonidas was sent to hold the narrow pass of Thermopylae, 80 miles (128 kilometres) north of Athens, against the advancing Persian army, so that the Persian fleet would be forced to fight the Greeks in order to clear a way round the coast to Athens (Plan 1). The channel between Euboea and the mainland was chosen as the best place to allow the manoeuvrability of the Greeks to outweigh the numerical superiority of the Persians.

In the event, the Persians suffered a setback even before they met the Greeks. Sailing down the Magnesian coast, they ran into a storm just as they were about to reach the safety of Aphetae, at the north end of the channel. Themistocles demanded an immediate attack, in the face of the almost unanimous caution of his fellow-commanders. The battle of Artemisium was indecisive but dramatic news arrived towards the close of the engagement. The Persian army had taken the pass of Thermopylae and was already marching towards Athens. Leonidas and his force had been betrayed and taken in the rear. The Spartans had died to a man.

Xerxes no longer depended on defeating the Greek fleet now that his army had broken through on land. The terrified Athenians evacuated their city, taking whatever belongings they could carry, while a small contingent fortified the Acropolis. Their efforts were to no avail. The Persians advanced to the city, sacked it and successfully stormed the Acropolis. Meanwhile the Greek fleet withdrew to Salamis and the Persian fleet rounded the southern tip of Attica to join up with the land forces.

It was essential for the Greeks to force another naval encounter on the Persians. Themistocles once again chose a narrow channel as the ideal battleground, the straits of the Bay of Eleusis, between the island of Salamis and the mainland. His problem was how to persuade the Persians to fight when it was no longer in their interests to do so. He also had to persuade his

A Greek trireme, showing the three banks of oars. This is similar to the ships used by the Greeks at Salamis.

fellow-commanders, including Eurybiades, that they must again make a stand, despite their worsening predicament. To accomplish both these ends, he resorted to a dangerous trick. He sent a secret message to Xerxes warning him that the Greek fleet was planning a hasty flight through the unguarded channel at the western end of the Bay of Eleusis and that this would be a good opportunity for Xerxes to catch the Greeks unawares and to smash them. Xerxes fell for the trick because he already knew that there was considerable disagreement between the Greek commanders and therefore found Themistocles' apparently treacherous message quite credible.

The Persian king at once ordered his Egyptian fleet of 200 ships to sail to the western entrance and block it. The rest of the Persian fleet formed a triple line between Piraeus (the port of Athens) and the promontory of Cynosura, on the island of Salamis. The channel at this end was divided by the small island of Psyttaleia, which left a threequarter-mile (1.2 kilometres) gap on either side. The Greeks dispatched their Corinthian allies to hold the Egyptians at the western channel and then ranged their ships in three groups between the town of Salamis and the mainland, to face the Persians (Plan 2). Themistocles led the Athenians with the majority of the fleet on the left flank, nearest the mainland. Eurybiades took the right flank with about sixteen ships. The rest of the Spartan and Athenian allies took the centre. So far, Themistocles' strategy to bring about a battle on water of his own choosing had worked perfectly. The trap was sprung. Now was the moment to see if Greek tactics could take advantage of the situation that had been created.

Unable to advance in their long lines because of the narrowness of the channel, the Persians split into two columns which sailed round either side of Psyttaleia. They at once lost their numerical advantage by sailing one behind the other in column. The rough sea, their own ineptitude and the lack of water in which to manoeuvre threw them quickly into some confusion. The Greeks sailed boldly into the chaos, shearing away the Persian oars and then turning to ram the ships themselves, forcing those in front back onto those behind.

It was Themistocles who achieved the decisive breakthrough. He sailed as close to the shore as he could and rounded the Persian right wing with his triremes, driving into the Phoenicians on the Persian flank (Plan 3). For a moment, there was a danger that Eurybiades' weaker wing would itself be turned by the Ionian left flank of the Persian fleet, but the success of Themistocles inspired the Spartans to greater effort. With Themistocles by then working round the Persian rear, the Ionians fell back. After 7–8 hours of hard fighting, the Persian fleet was beaten.

The reverse of a silver stater from Phaselis in Lycia, contemporary with Salamis. It shows the prow of a ship with a row of shields along the top. As the coin comes from Asia Minor, it probably represents the sort of ship that the Persians might have used. (Courtesy of Spink & Son Ltd, London)

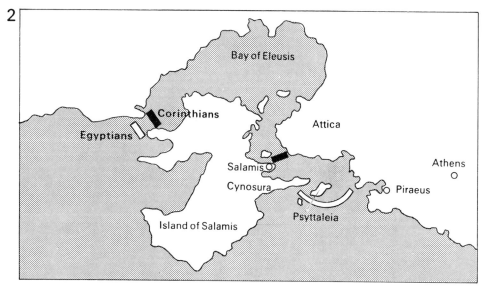

The Egyptians and the Corinthians face each other at the western entrance to the Bay of Eleusis while the main Greek force prepares to meet the Persian fleet in the narrow neck of water at the eastern end of the bay.

Greek soldiers, from a vase painting, arming themselves for battle.

The Greeks were in no fit state to pursue and the Persians still dominated the land, but the outcome of Salamis brought Xerxes' campaign to an end. Firstly, it was a blow to his prestige; secondly, it deprived him of the support of his transports and communications; and thirdly, it made him fear that his army would be cut off from its lines of retreat by the Greek fleet sailing north along the coast. He sent the remains of his fleet back east immediately and marched his army out of Greece. He, too, like Darius, had been turned back at what he thought was the moment of victory.

Themistocles (c. 514–449 BC)

The historian Thucydides called Themistocles an intuitive genius, brilliant at forward planning and quick to make the right decision in a crisis. Plutarch added that he was quite unscrupulous in getting what he wanted. A veteran of Marathon and rival of Aristides, he pushed through a policy of naval expansion and became the most important statesman in Athens (and probably in all Greece) after Aristides was ostracized in 482 BC. Following upon his victory at Salamis, he fortified Athens and the port of Piraeus and turned the city into the chief trading centre of Greece. But his high-handedness and great wealth alienated the Athenians. He later took refuge in Asia Minor, was welcomed by the Persians and died in Magnesia.

Impeded by the Island of Psyttaleia, the Persian fleet is forced to advance in two columns, on either side of the island. The major part of the Athenian fleet under Themistocles sails close to the shore and takes the Phoenician wing of the Persian fleet in the flank.

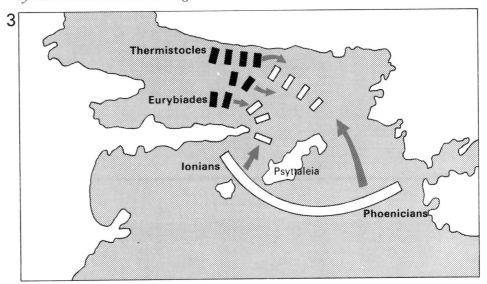

The Confederate town of Vicksburg, on the Mississippi, presented a major obstacle to Union forces during the American War between the States. Grant used the cunning of Themistocles and the dogged perseverance of MacArthur to outflank his enemy and attack their rear. He conducted a series of 'experiments' to keep them occupied, then distracted their attention by a feint in the north while he crossed the river further south and made a surprise flanking march, cut-off from his own supply lines.

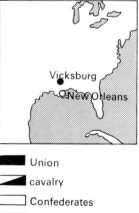

Ulysses S. Grant, commander of the Union forces at the siege of Vicksburg.

Abraham Lincoln became President of the United States of America in 1860 and, by the following year, those states were disunited and torn by civil war. Dedicated to freedom and determined to put an end to slavery, Lincoln also knew that America could not afford to be a divided nation, with north and south living to different patterns and codes. He had watched Europe exhaust itself by internal strife. When the southern states, one by one, seceded from the Union in pursuit of their own life-style, which included having black slaves, Lincoln was committed to keeping the Union intact. The ensuing struggle was between two opposing ways of life: the liberal, urban industrialists of the north and the rural slave-owners of the south. It seemed at first that the north had all the advantages. They had manpower, industrial wealth, arms and equipment and naval control of the seaboard. But the south, although ill-equipped, fought passionately for a cause in which they believed devoutly. They were more used to the rigours of outdoor life and coped better with the first months of tough campaigning.

The Confederate President, Jefferson Davis, was a match for Lincoln in the early stages of the war and was well-served by his senior commander, General Lee, who had at one point been asked to lead the Union forces. The south appeared to be gaining the upper hand in the first two years as the two sides thrust and parried in vain efforts to seize each other's capital—Richmond and Washington were only 100 miles (160 kilometres) apart. Superior numbers, equipment and wealth gradually increased the impetus of the north, whose army was forged into a victorious weapon with the emergence of General Grant as overall commander. At first, Lincoln had been too ready to replace his generals after any setback.

In the winter of 1862, it looked as if Grant, too, might lose the confidence of the President. The Confederate block against which he stumbled was the town

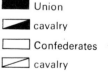

Union

cavalry

Confederates

cavalry

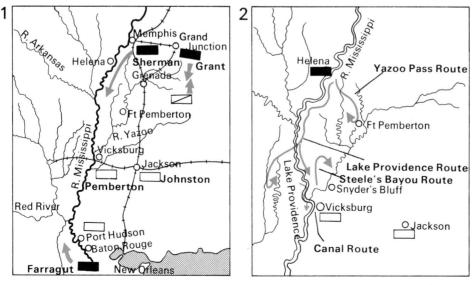

Far left: The original plan for taking Vicksburg failed. Grant was to go south by land while Sherman sailed downriver and Farragut sailed upriver. But the Confederates were dug in at Port Hudson, Vicksburg and Jackson and a cavalry force stopped Grant in the north.

View showing the river above and below Vicksburg, from a contemporary newspaper. Union boats are attempting the passage past Vicksburg.

Opposite page (2): Grant's experiments were partly to keep the Confederates guessing and partly to keep his own forces active during the winter. He tried four routes unsuccessfully: the Canal route, the Lake Providence route, the Yazoo Pass route and the Steele's Bayou route.

of Vicksburg, a stronghold on the Mississippi (Plan 1). Union river boats had been working their way south down the Mississippi in the preceding months, accompanied by forces on the land. In April 1862, Admiral Farragut had captured New Orleans from the Confederates and was able to sail his powerful steamers up the Mississippi from the south. But there remained a stretch of river between Vicksburg and Port Hudson, controlled by the Confederates, which stopped the Union forces joining from north and south. Vicksburg formed the vital bridge between the eastern and western halves of the Confederacy. Its capture would split the Confederacy and enable Grant's supply ships to have a free run of the Mississippi. This, in turn, would enable him to attack the Confederate forces from the east as well as from the north and from the western and southern seaboards.

There was another factor that made the capture of Vicksburg of great importance to the north. Many of the mid-western states relied on the Mississippi to provide transport for their harvests down to the Gulf of Mexico. Confederate control of the river cut off this outlet and forced them to pay exorbitant prices to move their goods either by rail or north through the Great Lakes. Seeking cheaper and easier alternatives, some of the states were threatening to secede from the Union for commercial and economic reasons. Grant had to free the Mississippi before they were forced into their fateful decision.

Grant's campaign was a protracted, frustrating affair that stretched over about six months and concluded with a wearying siege that finally reduced the town's garrison, under Pemberton, to surrender. Symptomatic of the looser, larger-scale battles that were common in the war and that became increasingly common in the 20th Century, the battle for Vicksburg nonetheless demonstrated Grant's tactical ability. For several months, he probed for possible weaknesses in Pemberton's defences and stretched his resources to the limit by constantly keeping him guessing as to the Union's next move. Having softened up his opponent, Grant then made a bold move at the opportune moment and achieved a marked success before the final siege by means of a flanking manoeuvre of remarkable daring.

Grant's initial plan was to march with an army overland from Grand Junction, north-east of Vicksburg, while his talented subordinate, Sherman, sailed downriver from Memphis and Farragut steamed upriver from New Orleans (Plan 1). This triple attack rapidly ground to a halt. Vicksburg was very well protected both naturally and with fortifications. The river meandered in great curves through swamps and tributary channels that made the surrounding countryside almost impassable to land-based troops except from the east. To the west, the river itself provided a barrier, made even stronger by earthworks on the Vicksburg bank. To the north, the marshes and the Yazoo River provided the basis for more defences, which proved impenetrable to the Union forces. To the east and south, the Confederates had dug themselves formidable earthworks, ditches and ramparts to guard against attack. Forced to abandon his approach from the north-east after two successful raids by Confederate cavalry who threatened his eastern communications, Grant had to consider how to attack Vicksburg from the north, west or south. If he was to attack from the south, he would have to pass downstream, through the Confederate batteries that guarded the Mississippi, or he would have to take an army down the western side of the river and cross back below the town. Every prospect looked equally hard.

The Union commander began a series of what he called 'experiments', partly aimed at keeping his own troops occupied during the winter months and partly aimed at keeping Pemberton guessing (Plan 2). Many of Grant's fellow-commanders commented that these 'experiments' looked rather more like 'failures', as indeed each proved to be in the first few months of 1863. One of the first was to dig a channel across the neck of the bend in the river on which Vicksburg stood. This would have enabled Grant to bypass the town. Unfortunately, the canal diggers were still within range of some of the Confederate batteries and eventually heavy rain destroyed their work completely. A more adventurous proposal entailed a long detour westwards from the Mississippi via a channel from the river to Lake Providence, and thence to the Red River, which in turn rejoined the Mississippi not far north of Port Hudson and well below Vicksburg. The first vessel that probed this route found the uncharted wastes of swamp unacceptably dangerous. The rising level of the water obscured the main channels and made shallows and sunken stumps a constant threat. This plan, too, was shelved.

The next two experiments involved attacks from the north. If Grant could not land his forces across the Mississippi, then he would try to find a favourable crossing point on dry land across the Yazoo River. The streams and bayous that

Grant in June 1864. His uniform was sometimes even less orderly than this. He was often stopped by guards who did not recognize him, because he was not in full uniform, and wanted to know what right he had to be wandering around the camp.

The end of the battle for another Civil War soldier: a contemporary photograph.

Far left: Sherman makes a feint across the river north of Vicksburg to distract attention from Grant's main crossing further south at Bruinsberg. Meanwhile the Confederates' confidence is shaken by Grierson's raid through to Baton Rouge.

Left: Cut off from his supplies, Grant makes a forced march south of Vicksburg towards Jackson. The Confederates are driven out of Jackson. At the same time Pemberton sends half his force south to cut Grant's non-existent supply lines. Finding nothing there, Pemberton marches north to Champion's Hill and is driven back to Vicksburg. The Union forces oust the Confederates from Snyder's Bluff and set about the long, final siege of Vicksburg.

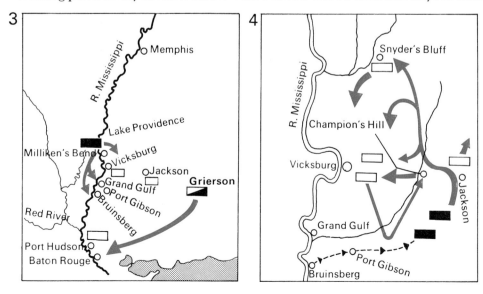

criss-crossed this area were particularly treacherous and confusing. It would also be necessary to go some way up the river to find a crossing point free from interference by the Confederates. One of Grant's plans was to reopen the levee on the eastern bank of the Mississippi, north of Vicksburg, at the town of Helena. This would provide access into the bayou known as the Yazoo Pass and thence, by a series of bayous and streams, to the Yazoo itself, at a point well above the formidable Confederate stronghold at Snyder's Bluff. A second experiment to avoid Snyder's Bluff was to sail up the Yazoo from the Mississippi, to turn off north just before the Bluff, up Steele's Bayou, and then by another series of twisting channels to reach the Yazoo again above the Bluff. In various ways, either by interference from Confederate troopers or by the impassability of the winding, overgrown streams, both routes failed.

The direct approach was the one that worked in the end. Grant decided to risk sending supply ships straight down the Mississippi, past the Vicksburg batteries, where only ironclads had passed before. It was a calculated risk but there seemed no alternative. Meanwhile McClernand led the Union army south, on foot, down the west coast of the Mississippi. With their vulnerable engine parts protected by bales of cotton and hay, the ships passed by at night. They received a severe battering but ran the gauntlet with success. These ships then enabled Grant and McClernand to bring the soldiers back across the Mississippi at Bruinsberg, at the very end of April, while Sherman made a feint attack north of Vicksburg to distract Pemberton's attention from the crossing (Plan 3). Simultaneously, Confederate confidence was shaken by a remarkable guerrilla raid by Grierson's Union cavalry, which rode from Tennessee through central Mississippi to Baton Rouge, below Port Hudson, on the river itself.

Grant had achieved a surprise crossing but he had still not attained his objective. No more ships were able to brave the batteries at Vicksburg and no supply ships were getting past the Confederate batteries at Port Hudson. The Union army was, in fact, cut off. Grant recognized that now was the time for his boldest move. He decided to forgo all attempts at keeping his supply lines open. Having seized Port Gibson and forced the Confederates to abandon Grand Gulf, Grant was joined by most of Sherman's force, which had marched down from Milliken's Bend and crossed the Mississippi at Grand Gulf. With more than 30,000 men, Grant left the river behind and marched inland. His soldiers carried their stores and equipment with them. It was Grant's intention to live off the land. On May 14, two of his commanders, Sherman and McPherson, struck north against the Mississippi capital of Jackson and drove the Confederate western commander, Johnston, out of the town (Plan 4).

Johnston was awaiting reinforcements and expected to have between 40,000 and 50,000 men within a week if Pemberton came out of Vicksburg to join him.

A battery of Union 32-pounders, from a contemporary photograph by the famous Civil War photographer Brady.

But Pemberton had orders from Jefferson Davis to hold Vicksburg at all costs. He therefore split his force (a fatal error) and moved south, with inadequate numbers, to cross the Big Black River in an attempt to cut Grant's supply lines from Grand Gulf. It was then he discovered that Grant had no supply lines. The Union commander's final 'experiment' had paid off. Pemberton hastened after him towards Jackson. On May 16, he met McClernand's force moving towards Vicksburg and was compelled to beat a hasty retreat after a struggle at Champion's Hill (Plan 4). His rearguard was broken up the next day and Sherman was able to seize Snyder's Bluff and Haynes's Bluff so that Union ships could sail up the Yazoo and resupply the Union army.

Grant immediately launched an assault on the town and was soundly beaten back. The defences of Vicksburg were still strong and the Confederates were by no means yet defeated. There followed a long siege in which the opposing engineers tried every trick of digging, mining and harassment. The Union forces had in addition to prevent Johnston from relieving the town. Exhausted and short of food and ammunition, 30,000 Confederates eventually surrendered on July 4. Terms were agreed in which Pemberton and his stalwart troops were not humiliated. As Grant himself said, he hoped that such terms would make the Confederates less dangerous foes and better citizens after the war. The Confederacy was split, the Mississippi was reopened and the subsequent victory at Gettysburg turned the tables convincingly against the south.

Ulysses S. Grant *(1822–1885)*

A veteran of the Mexican War, Grant resigned his commission to avoid court-martial for drinking and became an unsuccessful businessman. He rejoined the army at the beginning of the War between the States and made his name by defeating the Confederates at Shiloh in April 1862. After taking Vicksburg, he later became Supreme Commander of the Union forces, in the face of considerable opposition, and achieved a series of victories that reached their climax with the surrender of Lee at Appomattox in April 1865. He was elected President in 1868 and re-elected in 1872. Grant was primarily a strategist but was also a brilliant field commander who knew how to take calculated risks and to seize the tactical opportunities that his strategy prepared.

The siege of Vicksburg. The town is in the background and the Mississippi is just visible at the top right of the print.

Frederick the Great had already successfully used Grant's technique of false-footing his opponent by making a feint attack on one wing while he concentrated his forces to turn the other flank. In a manoeuvre directly descended from that of Epaminondas at Leuctra and Alexander at Gaugamela, the Prussians advanced obliquely against the Austrian left, routed it and attacked their centre from the flank. Frederick skilfully employed the 'refused' reserve cavalry of his oblique line to repulse a counter-attack.

Frederick the Great of Prussia, some years after his victory at Leuthen.

When Frederick II became King of Prussia in 1740, he was able to build on the foundations of State reorganization laid down by his two predecessors. Determined that Prussia was going to hold on to the advantages it had won at the end of the Thirty Years War, they had strengthened the Prussian army with the help of young officers from the noble, or Junker, class. Ruthless military training and constant battle drill had forged the army into the most disciplined force in Europe, with soldiers who were more afraid of their officers than the enemy. Frederick proved that he knew how to make the best use of this formidable military machine by his invasion of Silesia in 1740 and by the ensuing eight years of the War of Austrian Succession in which he held on to that territory.

The peace which came in 1748 was only temporary. War broke out again in 1756, with England subsidizing Prussia against the combined opposition of Austria, France, Russia and Saxony. Throughout the 'Seven Years War', Frederick's army was invariably outnumbered and he had to move swiftly to attack his enemies one at a time, before they joined forces. It was he who opened the war, with an undeclared strike against Saxony, which became the base for his future operations. He won a victory against the Austrians at Prague and then suffered two consecutive defeats in the same year, one by the Austrians at Kolin and one by the Russians at Gross Jagersdorff. The odds against him seemed overwhelming but Frederick persevered and in November 1757 was rewarded by the convincing victory of Rossbach against one Austrian army. The next month, he took the offensive against the other Austrian army under Prince Charles of Lorraine and Marshal Daun.

The Austrians had expected Frederick to go into winter quarters after his momentous victory and they were surprised by his continued advance. They came forward cautiously to meet him, leaving their heavy guns at Breslau and

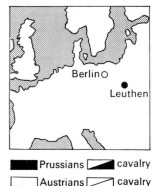

| Prussians | cavalry |
| Austrians | cavalry |

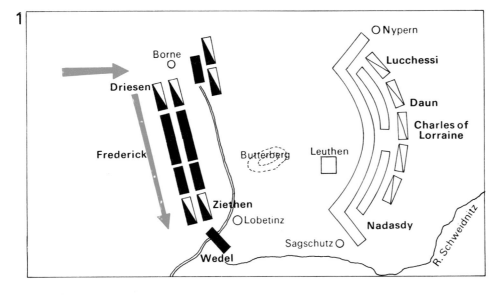

The Austrian army is drawn up behind Leuthen. The Prussians advance from the west and turn south-east to approach the Austrian left wing at an oblique angle.

Frederick began his Spring offensive in Bohemia in 1757 with a victory at Prague, illustrated here. He ended the year with his magnificent victory at Leuthen.

taking up a defensive position around the town of Leuthen. Their lines stretched for about 5½ miles (9 kilometres), from the small village of Nypern, on the right, to Sagschutz and the marshes along the River Schweidnitz, on the left. This line ran approximately north–south. Between 60,000 and 80,000 men were drawn up in two lines with cavalry reserves slightly behind. Lucchessi led the right wing, Nadasdy the left wing and Daun the centre (Plan 1).

Frederick had about 36,000 men, of whom about 12,000 were cavalry, which were placed on either wing of the infantry. Driesen was to lead the left wing, Ziethen the right and Frederick the centre. His plan of attack was worked out even before he met the enemy. He would feint at their right to persuade them to withdraw forces from their centre, then he would march across the line of their front and throw his full weight against their left, hoping to cut off their

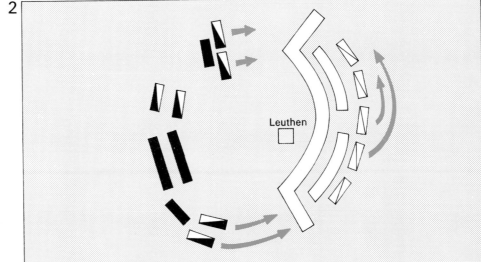

Frederick orders a feint attack on the Austrian right wing. Reserves of cavalry are hastily withdrawn from the Austrian centre and left to counter the threat, leaving the Austrian left weakened for Frederick's surprise flanking attack.

101

communications with Breslau, to the east. He later explained that an oblique attack was the obvious way for a small army to hit a much larger army: either it turned the enemy's flank with its concentration of force and defeated the enemy or, if defeated itself, then only the head of the column was routed and the remainder of the column could cover the retreat.

The Prussians approached in four columns from Neumarkt, to the west, on December 5, and encountered the first troops of the Austrian army while still on the march. This was a Saxon outpost at the village of Borne. The Saxons were immediately driven off and Frederick then wheeled his infantry south and re-formed them in two lines. They marched parallel to the Austrian front, hidden behind the brow of the hill, in perfect parade-ground order. At the same time, Frederick ordered a small feint attack by a section of the Prussian left wing. The Austrians were unable to see the main Prussian army. They were convinced, by the attack on Borne and by the feint, that the Prussians were about to attack their right wing. Lucchessi sent frantic messages to Marshal Daun to demand reinforcements for the expected assault. Daun sent all his reserve cavalry from the right as well as some of his reserves from the left. While these forces built up in the north and no immediate attack came, the Austrian centre was unsure whether the Prussians had now withdrawn or whether they should expect an attack along their front. Frederick had achieved the desired confusion (Plan 2).

At about midday, the Prussian columns reappeared between the villages of Lobetinz and Sagschutz. The Austrian defences of Sagschutz were charged by Wedel's leading infantry, with the support of a battery of six guns, followed up by more infantry under Prince Maurice of Orange. Nadasdy urgently requested reserves to counter the sudden attack on the Austrian left (the reserves were by then at the wrong end of the Austrian line) and made a brave counter-attack against Ziethen's Prussian cavalry. He succeeded in pushing them back for a time but then Ziethen rallied his squadrons and the Austrian left wing was put to flight. Pounded by artillery, the fugitives were pursued all the way from Sagschutz to Leuthen (Plan 3).

Maurice recalled the reserve cavalry from the right and, while he waited for them, he sent in his infantry to hold Leuthen. Pressed together in the confined area of the town, the Austrians fought from house to house in a desperate attempt to keep the Prussians out. It was a murderous struggle and only finally decided by the charge of Mollendorf's Prussian guards, which drove the Austrians from their last footholds. The whole battlefront had by then swung east–west, instead of north–south. The Austrians had established a battery of

A flintlock grenade discharger of about 1740, a dangerous-looking weapon that must have given quite a kick-back to the user.

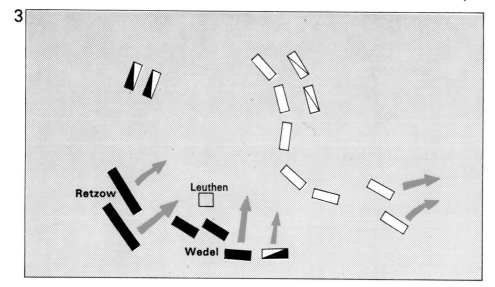

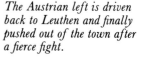

The Austrian left is driven back to Leuthen and finally pushed out of the town after a fierce fight.

guns above the town and were pinning down the Prussians who had taken it over. Frederick's reserve infantry, under Retzow, could make no headway against this battery so Frederick placed his own guns on the heights of Butterberg and over-pounded the Austrian battery and their infantry. Retzow eventually made a successful advance.

It was at this moment that Lucchessi saw Retzow's flank exposed and charged it with his cavalry. Frederick had already had to commit more of his reserves than he wished to, in his efforts to move forward from Leuthen, but he still had the cavalry of his left wing, which had so far 'refused' battle, being to the rear of his oblique line of advance. Driesen was waiting with forty squadrons behind the village of Radaxdorf. Under cover of the Butterberg battery, he galloped down on the busily occupied and unsuspecting Lucchessi (Plan 4). Lucchessi was killed and his troopers thrown back. Driesen then attacked the rear of the Austrian infantry in concert with a determined attack by Wedel's infantry in their front. Assailed from all angles, their resistance crumbled and they broke and fled towards Breslau. Frederick took Breslau on December 19 and confirmed his hold on Silesia. Prussian losses at Leuthen were approximately 1500 dead and 5000 wounded. The Austrians lost more than 20,000, including prisoners.

Napoleon called the Battle of Leuthen 'a masterpiece of movements, manoeuvres and resolution'. He claimed that Frederick's victory was by itself enough to immortalize him and to put him in the first rank of the great generals of history. He praised him in particular for his flanking march and for his surprise attack on the extreme left of the Austrians. But above all it was Frederick's tight control of his men and his total confidence in their ability to manoeuvre according to his plan that won him this impressive victory.

A typical 'blunderbuss' or flintlock of about 1740, a few years before Leuthen but there were almost certainly many in use at the time of the battle.

Frederick the Great (1712–1786)

When young, Frederick disappointed his disciplinarian father by preferring books and lute-playing to military training. He became King of Prussia in 1740 and his hard-headed realism then made itself apparent. He perfected the military machine that he inherited and planned his battles carefully in advance to provide him with a quick, decisive stroke rather than a slogging match, which his numerically inferior forces could never hope to win. His greatest victories were at Rossbach and Leuthen, within a month of each other, but the Seven Years War exhausted Prussia and he spent the rest of his life (more than 20 years) setting his State to order again. Napoleon provided his epitaph when he looked on his tomb in Potsdam: 'If he were still alive, we should not be here.'

As the Prussians continue their advance from Leuthen, Lucchessi attacks their exposed left flank but is himself taken by surprise by Driesen's cavalry and driven off. Driesen then attacks the rear of the Austrian infantry.

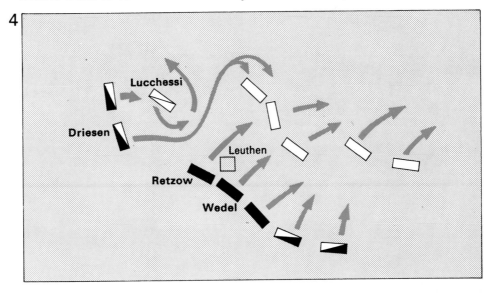

One of the most remarkable examples of a successful flank attack was achieved 100 years before Leuthen by the Great Condé in his first major battle, when still in his early 20s. An unintentional feint by the left of his French army saved him from a Spanish trap. He then attacked with his right, defeated the Spanish left and accomplished a cavalry charge around the rear of the enemy to attack their right flank from behind, taking them completely by surprise. The subsequent victory was a personal triumph.

The Great Condé, Louis II de Bourbon, after succeeding to his father's title. He was still the Duc d'Enghien when he defeated the Spanish at Rocroi.

The Duc d'Enghien, later to become famous as the Great Condé, was singled out at an early age by Cardinal Richelieu for his keen military intelligence and given command of the French army on the Flemish frontier in 1642. France was about to enter the Thirty Years War in strength. A few months later, Richelieu died and in May 1643, a Spanish army under the command of Don Francisco de Melo marched towards Paris from the north and set about the siege of the small town of Rocroi that stood in its way. Simultaneously, there was news of the death of Louis XIII and the accession of the child-king Louis XIV. France badly needed a decisive victory to bolster the new regime. D'Enghien therefore decided to fight a pitched battle to save Rocroi, against the advice of his cautious veteran counsellor, the Marêchal de l'Hôpital.

De Melo anticipated little trouble. He had an army of 20,000 infantry of mixed Spaniards, Italians, Germans and Walloons. The disabled but highly experienced Fontaine led the main Spanish contingent. De Melo also had 7000 cavalry, led by the famed Comte d'Isembourg and the Duc d'Albuquerque. He was confident of reinforcement by his German ally, General Beck, with 6000 more soldiers. The plateau outside Rocroi was about four miles (6.5 kilometres) wide, with woods, thickets and marsh surrounding it and only a narrow defile giving access to it. The Spanish army was drawn up on the plateau in its massed squares, or tercios (Plan 1).

D'Enghien advanced through the defile on May 17 but met with no opposition from de Melo until he reached the plateau. He led a total force of about 23,000 with rather fewer infantry than de Melo but approximately the same number of horse. De l'Hôpital himself commanded the infantry in the centre. The impetuous La Ferté Senneterre commanded the left wing of the cavalry and the right cavalry wing was commanded by the Comte de Gassion.

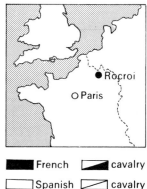

French ▮ cavalry ◣
Spanish ▯ cavalry ▨

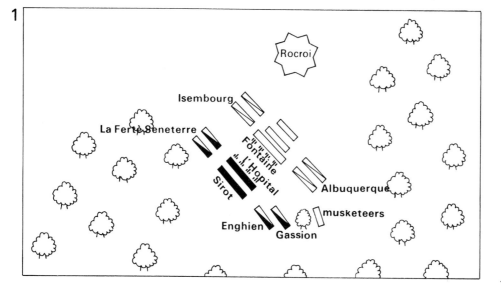

1

Rocroi

Isembourg
La Ferté Senneterre
Fontaine
l'Hôpital
Sirot
Albuquerque
musketeers
Enghien
Gassion

Left: The French and Spanish forces face each other on the open plateau outside Rocroi. De Melo's hidden musketeers lurk in the woods on his left wing.

Right: On the French right, Enghien and Gassion make a successful attack against Albuquerque. On their left, La Ferté's charge is quickly brushed aside by Isembourg, who then attacks the left flank of the French centre.

A musketeer with his match already burning and his musket shouldered, from the French Book of Arms of 1647, only four years after Rocroi.

Below right: A pikeman on the defensive against a cavalry attack, from the French Book of Arms of 1647.

D'Enghien also led a force of cavalry on the right wing, facing D'Albuquerque. He was ready to advance by the evening of the 17th, having decided that his best tactic was to try to turn the Spanish left wing. Little did he know that de Melo had prepared a trap for him on that very flank, in the woods to the east of the plateau through which D'Enghien must pass to attack D'Albuquerque. A hidden force of 1000 musketeers were ready to pour a devastating fusillade into the French cavalry.

In the event, the Spaniards were distracted and D'Enghien was saved by an unplanned incident on the French left wing. The over-cautious l'Hôpital had ordered La Ferté's cavalry forward to try to relieve the town and so avoid the necessity of a pitched battle. La Ferté advanced and was met by a massive charge from d'Isembourg's cavalry, which was only checked at the last minute because d'Isembourg had been expressly ordered by de Melo to avoid an immediate confrontation while the Spanish awaited the arrival of General Beck. De Melo's hesitation was a tragically missed opportunity and D'Enghien decided to defer the battle until the following day.

That night he learnt about the trap he had only just avoided. He was woken to hear from a deserter of the expected arrival of Beck, which he had not known about before. He also learnt from a picket in the wood of the presence of the Spanish musketeers. Ordering the army to be called to arms at three o'clock in the morning, he went back to sleep.

In the early dawn, D'Enghien mounted his horse and placed on his head a hat with huge white feathers that would enable his troops to pick him out easily in the coming fight. A preliminary engagement took place in the wood, where the Regiment of Picardy wiped out the musketeers. Then the Comte de Gassion rode in a wide arc to outflank D'Albuquerque's cavalry and to draw them away from the main line of the Spanish army. When he charged their first rank, it scattered quickly. D'Albuquerque rallied the second rank but they, too, were thrown back. Meanwhile D'Enghien had followed de Gassion closely with his own cavalry and made for the gap between the infantry and the remains of D'Albuquerque's wing. Taken on two sides, D'Albuquerque was driven from the field, with de Gassion in pursuit, while D'Enghien turned on the left flank of the infantry. It was then that he saw matters were not going so well on the other side of the field (Plan 2).

The incorrigible La Ferté had led a second, unauthorized attack on the Spanish right wing. D'Isembourg was waiting for him. The French cavalry were routed and their cannon were seized. D'Isembourg at once turned these cannon on the exposed left flank of the French infantry. L'Hôpital's troops

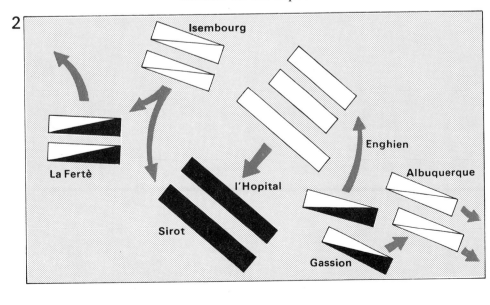

2

Isembourg

La Ferté

l'Hopital

Sirot

Enghien

Albuquerque

Gassion

managed to recover them once and then lost them again to a forceful advance by the Italian infantry, who turned the guns yet again on the French centre. It was only the firm stand made by the French reserve, under Sirot, that saved the centre from being completely broken at this point. This was the moment of decision for D'Enghien and he acted without hesitation. Sweeping round the rear of the enemy tercios (a manoeuvre in which he could have been cut to pieces if the squares had been able to turn rapidly enough to face him and cut him off), he launched his cavalry force at the Germans and Walloons in the rear of the Spanish army and then charged on to attack the Italians and D'Isembourg's cavalry on the right wing, which he put to flight. Sirot's men were vastly encouraged by the sight of D'Enghien's white plumes in the distance approaching from the other side of the enemy. But the battle was not over.

Cannon at the time of the Thirty Years War, probably similar to those used at Rocroi.

The main Spanish troops still stood firm and the chair-ridden Fontaine had two withering blasts of musket and cannon fire with which to greet the first two charges of the French. D'Enghien's cavalry had now recaptured the French cannon. It was essential that the Spanish formations were broken before the arrival of General Beck. The French preceded their third charge with a cannonade against one corner of the Spanish squares. There was no answering gunfire this time. The Spaniards had used up the last of their ammunition and the final French charge broke through the squares. La Fontaine himself was killed by a bullet and D'Enghien was hit and slightly wounded.

Several Spanish officers indicated that they would like to surrender. D'Enghien was about to receive them when some of the Spanish, alarmed that the attack had been renewed, opened fire with their muskets again. The infuriated French cavalry charged and began a massacre that was only stopped by the personal intervention of the French commander. The risk he took earned him the undying gratitude of the Spaniards he had defeated. Their losses were already very high. Some reports claimed that the total Spanish casualties were about 20,000, including prisoners. When General Beck eventually reached Rocroi, he saw what had happened and hastily withdrew.

Rocroi was a brilliant start to the Great Condé's career. His rapid attack round the rear of the enemy turned the fortunes of the encounter and gave him the advantage of surprise on the opposite flank. His tactical intelligence enabled him to make the best possible use of his Swedish-style cavalry (modelled on the cavalry of Gustavus Adolphus) against the ponderous Spanish-style squares.

The Great Condé (1621–1686)

The Duc D'Enghien was a prince of the royal blood and inherited his father's title to become the Prince of Condé, Louis II de Bourbon. He was known as the Great Condé. Appointed Governor of Burgundy at 17 and the commander of an army at 21, his victory at Rocroi was France's greatest for 100 years. He demonstrated his ability to make instant decisions closely based on the events of the battle in many subsequent victories, but suffered from the jealousies of Mazarin and spent much of his life fighting battles of tactical skill but of little international importance. In one battle, he had three horses killed under him and sat in the saddle for 26 hours with his feet in slippers because of gout. He retired a cripple but earned the eventual gratitude and respect of the King and continued to advise generals and statesmen till the end of his life. He was a considerate soldier and endeavoured to fight battles with the minimum loss of men.

D'Enghien's remarkable cavalry charge behind the Spanish lines, across the whole breadth of the field, drives Isembourg from the field and turns the tables on the Spanish infantry. The French attack with renewed vigour.

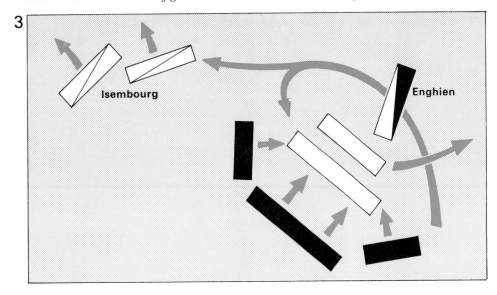

3

Isembourg

Enghien

Many tactical ploys, including the use of surprise as later demonstrated by the Great Condé, were fused together by the Byzantine commander Belisarius in a dazzling series of flank attacks that won him his greatest victory against the Persians. From a strong defensive position, he used carefully placed reserves to counter enemy attacks on both his flanks. He then turned to the offensive and used his final reserve to attack the exposed flank of the Persian centre and to confirm his superiority.

Detail from a mosaic at Ravenna, believed to be the head of Belisarius.

The Roman Empire in the west was overwhelmed by Vandals and Visigoths in the 5th Century AD and Rome itself ceased to be the centre of the civilized world. Byzantium took over the mantle of the Imperial capital and, renamed Constantinople, became the bastion of the Roman (and Christian) traditions. It was badly shaken at the beginning of the 6th Century by the onslaughts of the Persians on its eastern frontier. The Byzantines suffered several major defeats and were only saved from immediate disaster by an invasion of the Huns into Persia from the north. The distraction lasted only for a short time. The Persians had shaken off the Hunnish threat by about 525 and were once again troubling the Byzantine Empire. In a succession of minor engagements, the young Belisarius proved himself to be one of the rare successful Byzantine commanders. The Emperor Justinian was so impressed by his performance that he made Belisarius Commander in Chief of the Byzantine armies in the east before he was 30.

The traditional Roman armies of the west had made little use of cavalry, relying on their allies to provide whatever horse they required. But the eastern empire recognized the effectiveness of a strong cavalry force to provide mobility, fire-power and shock tactics. Their heavy cavalry were armed with lance or bow and often both rider and horse were covered in mail. These heavily armoured cavalry came to be known as 'cataphracts'. They were supported by light cavalry, who acted as skirmishers or probed for weaknesses in the enemy's flank and rear. They were also armed with bows. The light and heavy infantry were, on the whole, a subsidiary force who acted as the focal point or linchpin of the army. They were used either to cover the retreat of the cavalry or when the cavalry had already opened up a weak spot in the enemy defences or drawn the enemy into a vulnerable position. The heavy infantry fought in the traditional close-packed phalanx and were armed with long spears.

Byzantines cavalry
Persians cavalry

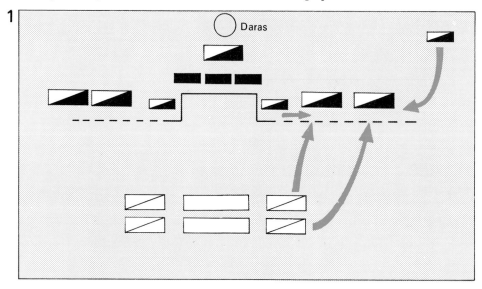

Belisarius positions his forces behind a defensive ditch, in front of Daras, with a reserve force of cavalry lying in wait in the hills on his left flank. When the Persian right wing crosses the ditch and attacks the Byzantine left, the Persian cavalry are surprised on both flanks.

The Byzantines built up a professional army with a solid structure and a rigid and logical chain of command. Tactics and strategy were studied conscientiously and several remarkable military texts were written over the centuries. Despite its relative numerical inferiority, this trusty war machine enabled the Byzantines to extend their empire under Justinian to include most of the eastern Mediterranean world and much of the western Mediterranean as well. It also ensured the survival of the Byzantine Empire against innumerable onslaughts (in particular by the Arabs or Moors) until the city itself fell in 1453. Much of this strength was established by Belisarius.

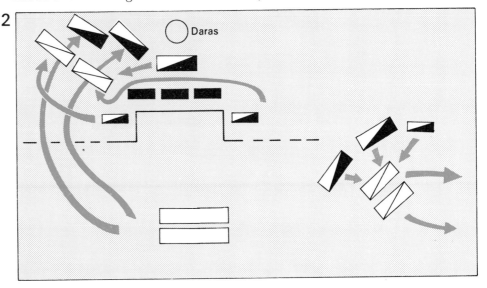

2

Daras

The Persian right is repulsed. On the left, the Persian attack also runs into trouble, taken in the flank and rear by reserves of Byzantine cavalry.

Justinian surrounded by his court, from the Ravenna mosaic. The figure on his right is thought to be Belisarius. There is a group of typical soldiers of the time on the extreme left of the picture.

In 530, a large Persian force of about 40,000 was bent on taking the frontier fortress of Daras, in northern Mesopotamia. Belisarius came to meet them with about 25,000 men. Like the Persians, a considerable proportion of his army consisted of cavalry. His infantry were mostly raw recruits who had not yet been battle-trained. Belisarius was determined to save the city but had no intention of allowing himself to be shut up in it for a long siege. He resolved to force a battle outside the walls, despite his numerical weakness. His plan was to prepare for a tactical defensive–offensive (like Alexander or later Wellington) and to establish his army in a reasonably secure defensive position, with his back to the walls of the city, from which he could take the offensive as soon as the opportunity arose.

To this end, he prepared a broad ditch in front of the walls and running parallel with them. At either end of this ditch, two more ditches were dug at right angles running forward. From the forward end of each of these ditches, the original line was extended to the protective hills on either side of the valley. These extensions were broken by several crossing points for the cavalry. The heavy cavalry were placed behind the extension arms of the ditch, on either flank, and a force of light cavalry were placed in both inside corners to harass the flank and rear of the enemy if they broke through. Belisarius also placed a force of light Hunnish cavalry in the hills on his left flank to provide a surprise attack. He tucked the untried infantry safely behind the main ditch and placed a final reserve force of heavy cavalry behind the infantry (his appreciation of the use of adequate reserves equalled that of Julius Caesar, Gustavus Adolphus or any modern commander). The infantry could in addition be protected by fire from the walls of the city itself (Plan 1).

The Persians also placed their infantry (javelin throwers, slingers and archers equipped with bows that were inferior to those of the Byzantines) in the centre of their line, in two massed rows, with cavalry on either flank. The Immortals (a hangover from the elite bodyguard used by Alexander the Great) took the left flank. On the morning after the arrival of the Persian army, Belisarius sent a message to the Persian commander suggesting that they might avoid a conflict if they got together and discussed their differences. He commented that peace was preferable to war and that the best general was the one who could bring peace about. The Persians looked at Belisarius's defensive ditch and interpreted his message as a further sign of Byzantine weakness. Confident that the Byzantines were psychologically beaten already, the

Persians attacked at once. They anticipated a quick and easy victory.

They avoided the strongly protected centre of the Byzantine line and first charged the Byzantine left, where they forced their way across the gaps in the ditch and pressed back the Byzantine cavalry. According to plan, the light cavalry inside the Byzantine wing then counter-attacked the left flank of the Persian cavalry and the Huns suddenly swept down from the hill and surprised the Persians on their right flank (Plan 1). Beset on three sides, the Persian right wing withdrew hastily.

The Persian left wing was more successful. The Immortals had also forced their way across the ditch and had pressed the Byzantines back to the walls of the city. But they advanced so fast and so far that they were completely cut off from the main Persian force. Belisarius seized his chance and sent both forces of light cavalry to attack the exposed rear of the Immortals. Simultaneously he sent his reserve force of heavy cavalry to attack their right flank (Plan 2). The previously hard-pressed right wing of the Byzantine army rallied and the Immortals were taken in front, rear and flank simultaneously. They were driven from the field, pursued by the now triumphant Byzantine right wing.

There was now a wide opening for Belisarius to attack the exposed left flank of the Persian centre. He took the offensive with his light cavalry and heavy reserve, emerged from behind his defensive ditch and charged the Persian infantry (Plan 3). His victory was quickly accomplished and completely decisive. The centre broke its formations and fled in scattered confusion. Daras was saved and Belisarius's tight control of the battle and sustained flexibility had proved his tactical ability. He had in fact demonstrated quite remarkable skill. He had made flanking attacks on both his enemy's wings and his centre from a defensive position and with a force half the size of his opponent's.

Belisarius (c. 505–565)

One of Justinian's most able commanders, Belisarius achieved his first great victory at Daras when he was only 25. In a succession of notable campaigns, he defeated the Vandals in North Africa, invaded Sicily, recaptured Naples and Rome from the Goths and defeated them at Ravenna in 540. He refused their offer to make him emperor and was recalled to the east by the jealous Justinian. He campaigned once again both in Persia and Italy and came out of retirement to drive off an invasion of Bulgars. Belisarius was first and foremost a brilliant field commander of cavalry. He insisted on stern discipline but was greatly admired by the motley collection of races within the army largely because of his unusual humaneness and his considerable list of victories.

A Byzantine soldier carrying a statuette of Victory, from a near-contemporary ivory relief now in the Louvre, Paris.

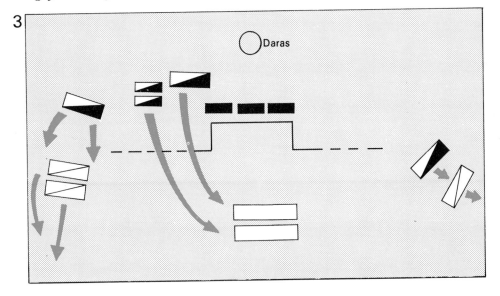

With the Persian cavalry driven from the field, Belisarius emerges from behind his defensive ditch to attack the helpless Persian infantry in its exposed flank. The Byzantine victory is complete.

The element of surprise has already been seen to play an important part in any tactical manoeuvre, whether in a direct, penetrating or flanking attack. The whole art of the commander is to catch his opponent off-guard by sudden or subtle movements. In some battles the carefully planned surprise attack plays a more than usually dramatic part. Gonzalo de Cordoba, known as the Great Captain, caught the French entirely unawares when he crossed the River Garigliano with his Spanish army.

The Great Captain, Gonzalo de Cordoba, from an early 16th-century German school of painting with strong Italian influences.

Warfare between the city states of 15th-Century Renaissance Italy had often been a stylized and artificial business, although always a cruel burden on the peasants of the countryside. It had been characterized by professional captains, or condottieri, like Francesco Sforza and Gattamelata (the 'honeyed cat'), who gathered about them bands of mercenaries and hired themselves out to the highest bidder. When battle was joined, it could be fierce and bitter but treason and murder were the more common methods of achieving political ambitions. Cesare Borgia was the archmaster of such manoeuvres.

France entered this incestuous arena with heavy artillery and ruthless determination at the end of the century. Charles VIII invaded Italy and spent a year upsetting the unsteady equilibrium of the city states. His successor, Louis XII, seized Milan from the unfortunate Ludovico Sforza (son of Francesco), who had first invited the French into Italy, and Louis's soldiers practised their archery on the great equestrian model of Ludovico built by Leonardo da Vinci.

Spain, only recently united under Ferdinand and Isabella and freed at last from the Moors, looked on France's interference in Italy with great suspicion. Both Ferdinand and Louis laid claim to Naples but neither wanted to come to blows. They put on a bland face of co-operation. When the Ottoman Turks launched a major threat on Italy in 1500, Ferdinand sent a strong army under his chief captain, Gonzalo de Cordoba, to reinforce the French. He also thought that it would be no bad idea to have an army in readiness to smother Louis's ambitions. The Ottomans were turned away and Louis and Ferdinand then made an agreement to divide the Kingdom of Naples between them. Neither had much intention of keeping to the agreement once Naples had been seized. The French quickly overran the agreed dividing line and, by 1502, France and Spain were at war in Italy. The next year, Gonzalo de Cordoba won two convincing victories against the French at Cerignola and Garigliano.

■ Spanish
□ French

1

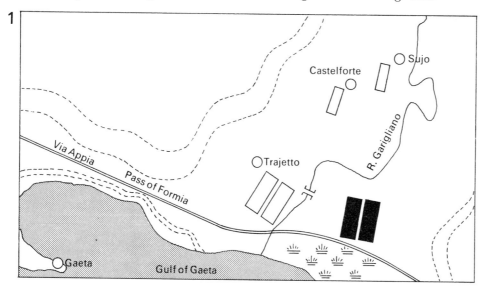

The French and Spanish armies face each other across the River Garigliano. The Spanish were determined to stand between the French and Naples.

The most common name for the handgun fitted with a matchlock was the arquebus. This triple-barrelled matchlock is from the arsenal of the Emperor Maximilian I, who died in 1519. Nicolaus Glockenthon illustrated all the weapons in the arsenal in three volumes, about 1505.

Below: The suit of armour worn by Gonzalo de Cordoba. In the damp conditions that preceded the final battle at Garigliano, great care would have had to be taken to keep armour rust-free and in good repair.

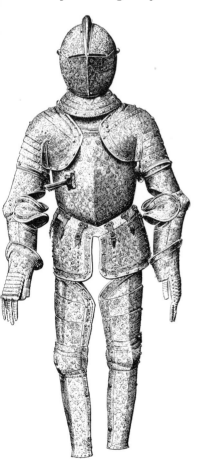

One of Gonzalo's greatest achievements was a realization of the value of the infantry soldier armed with a handgun. The handgun, in the form of the arquebus, was only just emerging as a practical weapon. In its early stages, it had been a cumbersome object, which generally had to be fired by two men (one to support it) and required the application by hand of a burning match to ignite the gunpowder. It is not hard to imagine the peril of this practice and the inefficiency of the subsequent shot. The handgun had sensibly been used with circumspection. Towards the end of the 15th Century, certain improvements changed its character and greatly added to its usefulness. It was made lighter—although it could still weigh 30 lb (13.6 kilos). It was also made more accurate, with a longer barrel and a smaller calibre. The most welcome change was the matchlock, which made ignition of the gunpowder automatic: a burning match was fixed to the gun and came down on the gunpowder pan when the trigger was pulled. The arquebusier could therefore concentrate his aim without having to manipulate the burning match at the same time.

The arquebusiers were backed by pikemen, to protect them as they reloaded, and accompanied by light cavalry to harass and pursue the enemy. Gonzalo believed that his arquebusiers were the equal of any of the conventional forces of the time: pikes, crossbows or cavalry. At Cerignola he showed that he knew how to use them. He lured the French pikemen and footsoldiers on to his thin line of waiting arquebusiers and fired several steady rounds at close quarters before advancing his own pikemen from behind the line to rout the enemy.

Revived by reinforcements, the French then marched down the coast to capture Naples but Gonzalo cut across in front of them and faced them over the estuary of the River Garigliano (Plan 1). The French army was almost double the size of the Spanish army. The troops were fresher, well-fed and well-paid. But it was already November, one of the worst Novembers in memory, and torrential rains had swollen the river and turned the surrounding banks into a quagmire. The French found the conditions intolerable. It was a superb chance for Gonzalo to show his superior skill as a tactician and a commander.

113

The French tried at first to throw a pontoon over the river but were frustrated by the fast-flowing water. They gained a temporary foothold on the far bank and forced the Spanish back but, with the effective use of their arquebus fire (when the rain allowed) and the appalling mud, the Spanish eventually persuaded the French to withdraw to their side of the river. Gonzalo was in no hurry to continue the fighting. His plan was to let the French suffer miserably in the downpour, while he awaited his opportunity to attack. Meanwhile he kept up the spirits of his own men by visiting their lines daily.

The waiting game lasted for six weeks. The French officers found the bankside camp too uncomfortable and retired to cosy billets in farmhouses and villages well back from the line. Even the commanding general found an excuse to be replaced. Despite their resources, the French also found it increasingly difficult to acquire adequate supplies and provisions, as the countryside around them became rapidly exhausted by the demands of their army. The soldiers themselves edged further and further back from their forward positions along the bank, in an attempt to find dry accommodation.

On Christmas Day, soldiers from both sides joined together in seasonal celebrations, welcoming the bright relief from their discomfort. Nothing was further from French thoughts than battle. It was time for Gonzalo to make his move. He had already prepared a pontoon bridge which could be carried in sections to a crossing point higher up the river. He moved two days after Christmas, leaving a rearguard, under Andrada, to deceive the French into believing that the Spanish were in their usual positions. With a vanguard under Alviano and a strong centre under his own command, Gonzalo crossed secretly to the village of Sujo, on the French left (Plan 2).

Alviano's light cavalry attack on December 29 was completely unexpected. He swept through the French wing, brushed aside the Swiss pikemen and launched himself against the centre of the French army, under their commander, the Marquis of Saluzzo. Taken by surprise, the resistance was minimal and Saluzzo withdrew along the Via Appia to take a stronger stand in the narrow pass at Formia (Plan 3). Andrada also crossed the river to join the fight and there was a fierce struggle for an hour before the French had enough.

Many were subsequently trapped in Gaeta, at the end of the small peninsula. Others fled to Rome, harassed by the peasants and stripped of their possessions and even their clothes. More than one contemporary remarked on the extraordinary sight of naked Frenchmen seeking out the dunghills of the city and burying themselves there for warmth. Several hundred were found dead on the dunghills the following morning.

A medal struck after the death of Gonzalo de Cordoba to commemorate his victories.

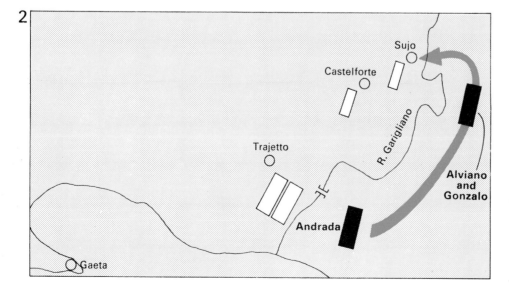

Gonzalo's stamina and patience tell in the end. The weary French are lulled into a sense of security and then Gonzalo makes a surprise crossing of the river upstream and catches them in their flank.

A facsimile of an ancient engraving of a battle scene of about 1495, less than ten years before Garigliano. Pikemen supported by cannon and a few handguns drive off the traditionally superior armoured knights.

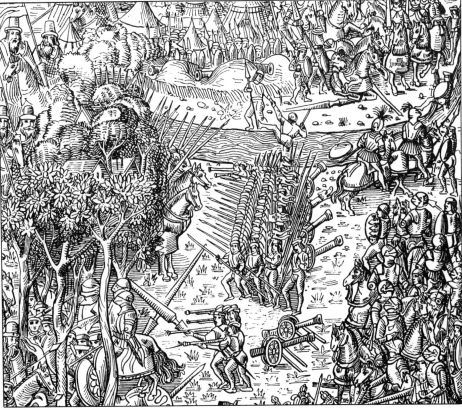

Gonzalo de Cordoba (1453–1515)

Born in the year that Constantinople finally fell to the Turks, 'The Great Captain' was the outstanding commander at the turn of the century and greatly influenced the shape of warfare in the future by his emphasis on the use of the handgun. He made his name in driving out the Moors from southern Spain and demonstrated his skill by his tactical speed and adaptability. His victories in Italy incurred the jealousy of Ferdinand, who recalled him to Spain in case he took Naples for himself. When Gonzalo ordered the construction of a giant crossbow for one of his campaigns, he had it decorated with a highly suitable inscription: 'Cleverness overcomes strength.' He died of malaria contracted in Italy.

The Spanish are quickly driven back along the Via Appia. They make an unavailing stand at the narrow pass of Formia. Then they retreat again, broken and in confusion.

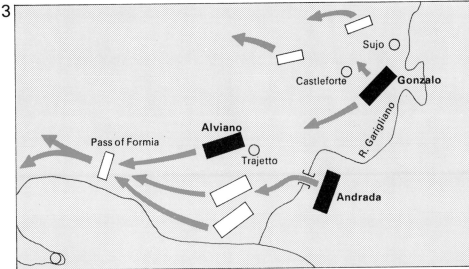

Johan Baner was a veteran of the Swedish victory at Breitenfeld. In his own courageously planned victory at Wittstock, five years later, he used surprise against his Imperialist enemies as effectively as the Great Captain had at Garigliano. With a small force, he held the attention of their entire army by a brave attack on one flank while the other half of his army made its way secretly behind the Imperialists. The plan relied on perfect timing and the timing very nearly went wrong.

Johan Baner, the brilliant cavalry leader and victor of the Battle of Wittstock.

The victories of Gustavus Adolphus at Breitenfeld and Lutzen appeared to be the peak of Sweden's military achievement during the Thirty Years War. The second victory cost the king his life. Two years later, the Swedes suffered a heavy reverse at Nordlingen. Their model army was smashed and they lost their hold in southern Germany to the Spanish-Imperialists. John George of Saxony, who had fought (and fled) on the Swedish left wing at Breitenfeld, joined the Emperor and turned against his former ally. Only Richelieu's active support kept the Swedes in the war.

After Nordlingen, Johan Baner was appointed overall commander of all the Swedish forces in Germany. His first task in his new command was to restore discipline and revive morale in the Swedish troops. He took severe action against incipient mutineers and resolved to force a battle with the Imperialists as quickly as possible in an energetic effort to regain the ascendancy. To this end, he was joined by Torstensson, another veteran of Breitenfeld, who later succeeded Baner to overall command.

John George and the Imperialist forces under Hatzfeld and Morazini confidently aimed to cut between Baner and his line of retreat to the Baltic. They anticipated reinforcements from Brandenburg. Baner needed to move between John George and the Brandenburg contingent before the reinforcements augmented the Imperialist army. The Swedes caught their enemy up near the town of Wittstock, on the River Dosse, a tributary of the Havel. The Imperialists took up a strong defensive position on a ridge that faced south and south-east, with the town behind them (Plan 1). Hatzfeld commanded the Imperialist right wing, facing directly south. Morazini also faced south in the centre. The Saxons were placed on the left wing and faced south-east, so that the whole line curved round towards that end. Between the Saxons and the

Swedes ▮ cavalry ◤
Imperialists ▭
cavalry ◪

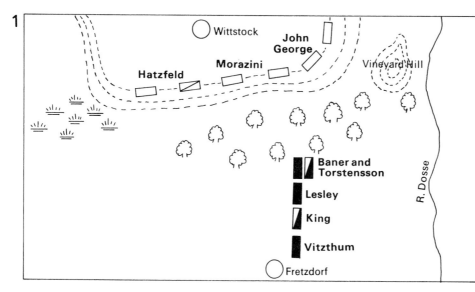

1

The Imperialists take up their positions on the curved hill facing south and south-east, with the town of Wittstock behind them. The Swedish army advances from the south.

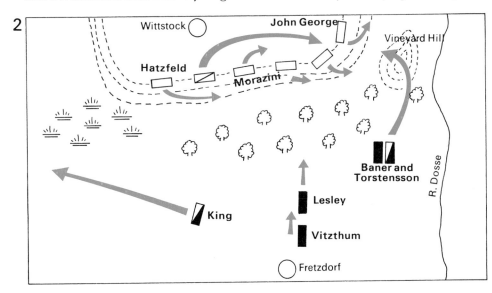

The Battle of Wittstock, from a print of 1695. With the town in the background, this could be the moment when Lesley brought up his infantry to attempt to support Baner's initial cavalry attack.

River Dosse was a prominent mound, known as Vineyard Hill. The slope below the Imperialist position on this side was well-protected by trees and undergrowth that made it hard to assault. The woods continued along the slope in front of the centre of the Imperialists, where Morazini had also prepared very thorough earthworks. Hatzfeld's flank was protected by a marsh.

It was a daunting prospect for the Swedes. They were also outnumbered. The combined Saxon-Imperialist force contained thirteen infantry brigades and more than seventy cavalry squadrons, with a total of about 20,000 men. The Swedes had nine infantry brigades and about fifty cavalry squadrons, with

Baner and Torstensson advance to Vineyard Hill to draw the attention of the Imperialists, while King makes a detour around Hatzfeld's flank to make a surprise attack in the rear.

a total of 15,000 men. Besides Torstensson, Baner had two Scottish generals, Lesley and King, and a rearguard commanded by Vitzthum.

Advancing north from Fretzdorf, about 4½ miles (7 kilometres) to the south of Wittstock, Baner worked out a daring plan to take the initiative against the strong opposition and superior numbers of the opposing allies. He would split his army into two separate forces that would, he hoped, join up at the right moment to take the Imperialists on several sides simultaneously. Baner and Torstensson were to advance on the right, seize Vineyard Hill and force the allies to turn their attention to face this threat. Lesley, meanwhile, would advance straight ahead to protect the left flank of Baner's force, in case it should be surrounded on Vineyard Hill. At the same time, King, with half the cavalry, would make a wide sweep to the left, around Hatzfeld's wing, and take the Imperialists in the flank and rear (Plan 2). Baner was in effect setting himself up as bait. The success of the plan depended on the timing of Lesley and King's support. In the event, the timing was almost disastrous.

The woods along the slopes at first gave the Swedes an advantage. King's movement to the left was never seen and Baner and Torstensson were able to advance under cover to Vineyard Hill. They seized it quickly and immediately drew the enemy attention—and fire. Hatzfeld sent cavalry reserves from his own wing (as Baner had hoped he would) and the seventeen squadrons of the Swedes soon found themselves fighting to hold off about fifty Imperialist squadrons (Plan 2). (The Saxons had barely outlasted Baner's first attack, showing as little spirit as they had at Breitenfeld.)

The Imperialists then began to build up the pressure on Baner with infantry reinforcements from their centre. With no sign of Lesley's support and as yet no signal from King that he had completed his encirclement, Baner's plan appeared to be turning against him. He sent urgently to find out what had happened to Lesley and to call up the reserves under Vitzthum, who seemed unaccountably reluctant to respond with any speed. Delayed by a series of accidents, Lesley arrived just when Baner was about to be enveloped. Lesley held off the Imperialist infantry but was then himself subjected to a charge by Hatzfeld's cuirassiers and suffered severe losses. His support on Baner's flank was clearly insufficient. Baner was being forced back down Vineyard Hill and there was still no sound of King.

King had his own problems. The marshy ground on the Imperialist right had proved an impassable obstacle to his cavalry and he was forced to make a detour of about 6–7 miles (10–11 kilometres) to reach his objective. It took him the best part of the afternoon to achieve this. Evening was falling and Baner was giving up hope when at last he heard the long-awaited signal that King had outflanked the Imperialists. Vitzthum appeared through the woods at almost the same time and the tables were suddenly turned on the Imperialists (Plan 3).

Above and right: A pikeman of the time of Wittstock going through his exercises with his none-too-easy-to-handle weapon. The final position is exactly the same as that taken up by the pikeman illustrated in the Battle of Rocroi, seven years later.

Below: A mounted arquebusier or 'bandolier rider' of the Thirty Years War. The presence of the ever-burning match must have done little to calm the nerves of the horse when in action.

Taken completely by surprise by King on their right, and pressed by Baner, Vitzthum and Lesley on their left and centre, they were caught in the riskily prepared trap. Their right flank, which King attacked, had in fact become their rear, as their entire line had been turned to the left to annihilate Baner and Lesley. They turned to retreat, were caught up in the confusion and panicked. In a remarkably short time, what had appeared to be an Imperialist victory had been transformed into a rout. Standards, stores, weapons and cannon were abandoned. The Imperialist infantry were cut down in large numbers during the vigorous pursuit that followed.

Baner's victory restored Sweden's failing reputation and her position in Germany. The upset of Nordlingen was forgotten and many of the north German princes who had been prepared to give up the struggle and make their peace with the Emperor took new heart. Saxon influence was badly shaken and Brandenburg was retaken by the Swedes. After further ups and downs of fortune, the combined military efforts of France and Sweden concluded in the Peace of Westphalia that brought an end to the Thirty Years War in 1648. It was a peace that the two powers guaranteed to 'protect'.

Few commanders in the war would have been prepared to take the risk that Baner did at Wittstock, although he based his plan on classic principles. He determined to dictate the manner in which the battle should be fought; he forced the enemy into an error by encouraging them to strengthen their left at the expense of their right; and, by capturing their complete attention with only a proportion of his army, he was able to take them by surprise with a substantial force in flank and rear. The near-failure of his plan, through unforeseen circumstances, demonstrated the fickleness of war and proved that his decision was not only brilliantly planned but also courageous.

Johan Baner (1596–1641)

A great admirer of the military innovations of Gustavus Adolphus, Baner led the right wing of the Swedish army at Breitenfeld and then became Gustavus's chief of staff. He was later wounded and did not take part in the Swedish victory at Lutzen. His greatest victory was as commander of the Swedish army at Wittstock. Subsequently he was forced to retreat into northern Germany but re-emerged with reinforcements and gained new victories: 'The enemy had put him in the sack but forgotten to tie it.' He died of a pulmonary disease. Baner's tactics were based on speed of manoeuvre and a desire to seize the initiative. He was one of the most original commanders in the Thirty Years War and Sweden owed its recovery in the mid-Thirties largely to his efforts and skill.

The Imperialists suddenly face a combined attack on several fronts simultaneously. King has rounded their flank and Vitzthum has eventually arrived from the south. Baner, Torstensson and Lesley turn on the offensive.

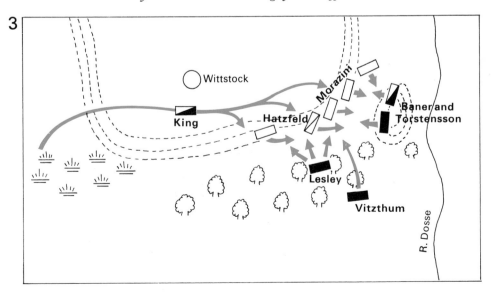

The surprise attack has been achieved with outstanding success in the 20th Century as well as in the smaller battles of earlier centuries. During the Allied counter-offensive in Burma, General Slim deceived the Japanese into believing that his entire army was crossing the Irrawaddy to attack Mandalay. One army corps advanced unseen by the Japanese to cross the river further south and to surprise Meiktila. Caught between two attacks, it was the beginning of the end for the Japanese in Burma.

Lieutenant-General Sir William Slim, commander of the Fourteenth Army in Burma.

The Japanese had invaded Burma in January 1942. They took Rangoon on March 7 and moved rapidly north to the historic city of Mandalay by the end of April, driving the British forces back into India. They halted only when they reached the River Chindwin. It was a hard, tiring retreat for the British and there followed a considerable period in which they recouped their strength and retrained their men. During 1943 Mountbatten took over as Supreme Commander South-East Asia and late in the year Slim took over as commander of the British Fourteenth Army. While this army made tentative probes into the coastal area of Arakan and Chinese–American forces probed from the north-east under Stilwell (and subsequently under Wedemeyer), Orde Wingate's Chindits attempted to disrupt the Japanese supply lines during 1943 and 1944.

In March 1944, the Japanese Fifteenth Army, under Mutagachi, crossed the Chindwin and advanced to Imphal and Kohima (Plan 1). There followed a three-month struggle before Imphal was finally relieved. The Japanese were pushed back east of the Chindwin with an incredible loss from battle and disease of about 65,000. Taking advantage of the weakened Japanese position, Stilwell began an offensive in North Burma to seize the Burma Road. In November 1944, Slim prepared his own offensive to recapture Mandalay and return to Rangoon.

Operation Capital was intended to catch the Japanese on the open plain, west of Mandalay, where Slim's superior armour (the Japanese tanks were becoming neglected) could crush the Japanese with the help of the Allied airforce. Slim then had about nine divisions against about four divisions under General Kimura. But once the Fourteenth Army had crossed the Chindwin the Japanese withdrew rapidly to take up a strong position on the Irrawaddy and at Mandalay. Slim promptly adapted his plan to Operation Extended Capital, the purpose of which was to approach Mandalay from two entirely different directions, while deceiving the Japanese as to his real intentions (Plan 2). XXXIII Corps, under Stopford, was to attempt a crossing of the Irrawaddy near Mandalay, in the north, while IV Corps, under Messervy, was to creep stealthily south and then cut east to cross the river near Pakokku. IV Corps' objective was Meiktila, the centre of Japanese administration in the area and of several airfields and railway junctions. The intention was to cut Kimura off from this vital supply base and then to catch his army between XXXIII Corps and IV Corps.

The key to the plan was surprise; the main problem was supply. It was an enormous task to keep IV Corps supplied in secret, without the Japanese being aware of its movements, a task compounded by the difficult jungle conditions. The solution of this administrative headache was as much to Slim's credit as the cunning of his basic plan. It was not enough that IV Corps should simply vanish into the jungle. That would have made the Japanese highly suspicious. A dummy Corps HQ was established and every effort was made to give the appearance that IV Corps was still about to attack from the north, alongside

XXXIII Corps. IV Corps itself maintained complete radio silence. Although the secrecy of their movements was helped by Allied air supremacy, Slim suffered a setback when a considerable part of his air support had to be withdrawn before the battle. He was lucky: when the Japanese did spot occasional lines of vehicles heading through the jungle, they did not consider them to be major troop movements, so convincing was the imaginary presence of IV Corps' HQ in the north.

Stopford's XXXIII Corps moved forward on Christmas Eve 1944. By January 14, 1945, they had established two bridgeheads on the east side of the Irrawaddy, north of Mandalay, at Thabeikkyin and Kyaukmyaung. A third bridgehead was established subsequently to the west of Mandalay. This convinced the Japanese that the main attack would come against Mandalay and they confidently began to mass their forces there, even, as Slim had hoped, bringing up forces from Meiktila. The fighting became particularly fierce over the next three weeks.

Meanwhile Messervy was moving down the bullock track up which Slim had retreated in 1942. IV Corps also used timber boats to bring supplies along the river. Messervy's target date for crossing the Irrawaddy was February 14, by which time it was judged that Stopford in the north would be hard pressed to hold his position. IV Corps reached the Irrawaddy valley at the end of January and prepared airstrips and reception areas for supplies and tanks. The river was more than a mile (1.6 kilometres) wide in many parts and Messervy found the narrowest crossing point (about 1 mile across) opposite Nyaungu, a little

Under enemy fire and with fire burning all around them, soldiers of the Fourteenth Army attack towards Mandalay.

south of Pakokku. Not content with this, he prepared two dummy crossing points, one at Pakokku itself, where tanks were to be used to give the impression that this was an important point, and the other about 40 miles (64 kilometres) south at Seikpyu. He also made a smaller feint at Pagan.

The main crossing was made at Nyaungu before dawn precisely on February 14. It was made completely silently, without preliminary artillery or air cover. Despite temporary confusion and setbacks, a bridgehead of two brigades was established by the 16th. The tanks had been ferried across on extremely vulnerable-looking rafts. Caught entirely by surprise, the Japanese rallied their resistance but Messervy had unwittingly chosen the perfect place to land. Nyaungu formed the dividing line between the Japanese Fifteenth and Twenty-eighth Armies and there had been some dispute as to whose responsibility the village was. It was temporarily held by the relatively unenthusiastic Indian National Army. Within 48 hours of the crossing, XXXIII Corps achieved another bridgehead in the north at Myinmu, once again distracting Kimura's attention. Convinced that the whole of the Fourteenth Army was still in the north, he called up more reserves and built up his forces to nearly double the strength of XXXIII Corps.

Messervy's motorized spearhead, under Cowan, made a dash for Meiktila. In danger of being trapped by the remaining Japanese forces, it was saved by Allied air supplies and Meiktila was captured against stiff Japanese resistance by March 3. The fall of Meiktila threw Kimura completely off-balance. Scrapping his plans for a major counter-attack against Stopford's Corps, he turned his attention south (Plan 3). Messervy's Corps was attacked simultaneously by the Japanese Fifteenth Army from the north and the Twenty-eighth Army from the south. It was their turn to hold Kimura's attention while Stopford's Corps launched their own major offensive against Mandalay.

IV Corps repulsed the Japanese attacks by a series of rapid sorties in small groups and cut them off before they got too close. They also relied heavily on air support. The Japanese were steadily pushed back. Meanwhile, at Mandalay, Japanese resistance took on a desperate, last-ditch toughness. They used human mines to destroy tanks. Soldiers crouched in fox-holes, gripping the firing pin of aircraft bombs and waiting for the tanks to pass. But even these measures did not save the Japanese from defeat. By the third or fourth week in March, both Mandalay and Meiktila were securely in the hands of the Fourteenth Army. The daring switch of Messervy's entire Corps across a 300-mile (480-kilometre) front had paid off. The British reached Rangoon on May 2. Slim had shown himself a master of mobility.

■ British Fourteenth Army

□ Japanese

Far left: The Japanese Fifteenth Army crosses the Chindwin in March, 1944, and advances against Imphal and Kohima. After three months of struggle the Japanese are pushed back.

Left: Operation Extended Capital was a two-pronged attack against Meiktila and Mandalay. XXXIII Corps, under Stopford, crossed the Irrawaddy north and west of Mandalay, while IV Corps secretly switched from north to south and made a surprise attack against Meiktila.

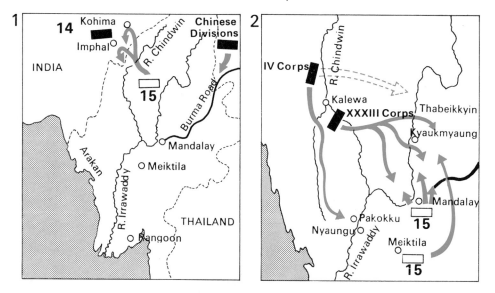

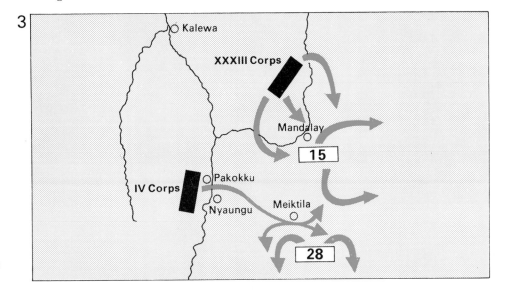

Above: General Slim at the Headquarters of the 4th Brigade, studying a plan of the campaign with Brigadier R. S. McNaught.

Above right: Sherman tank and troops of the Fourteenth Army cross the Irrawaddy on their way to Meiktila and Mandalay.

Field Marshal Slim (1891–1970)

Commissioned from the ranks in the First World War, Slim commanded a brigade at the outbreak of the Second World War. He was a corps commander in the 900-mile (1440-kilometre) British retreat before the Japanese in Burma in 1942. As commander of the Fourteenth Army, he successfully defended Imphal and Kohima in 1944 and counter-attacked to achieve a major victory at Meiktila in March 1945. With the use of fast-moving columns supplied from the air, he retook Rangoon and, by May, had driven the Japanese out of Burma. This was a remarkable military achievement. His reputation as a soldier and as a man has always been high. He was greatly admired both by his colleagues and his men.

The Japanese turn their attention to Meiktila, where IV Corps is attacked from the north by the Fifteenth Army and from the south by the Twenty-eighth Army. The distraction enables XXXIII Corps to launch a major offensive against Mandalay and the Japanese are finally driven out of both towns.

Both Slim and Baner had distracted their opponents' attention by advancing on one flank of their position and surprising them with a sudden attack on the other flank. The Mongol commander Subedei accomplished much the same feat but first he lured his Hungarian victims forward, through thick snow, into his carefully prepared trap. It was the tactic that won Salamis and Austerlitz and almost won Kadesh. The dramatic charge by Subedei's Mongol horde threatened to encircle the terrified Hungarians.

Portraits of the Mongol commander Subedei are virtually non-existent but we can catch something of his positive and confident character in this portrait of his overlord, Ogedei, son and immediate successor of Genghis Khan.

Christian Europe saw the Mongol invasions of the 13th Century as a visitation from Hell. They faced the elusive horsemen and the murderous clouds of arrows with the proud chivalry of Templars, Hospitallers and Teutonic knights but the might of Christendom was crushed and swept aside with skilfully organized efficiency. In two great battles, at Wahlstadt (near Liegnitz) and at Mohi Heath, on the River Sajo (not far from Gran, now Budapest), Mongol mounted tactics proved that mobility and firepower were the absolute masters of the badly co-ordinated western forces of infantry and heavily mounted knights. Only the death of the Great Khan, Ogedei, and the subsequent withdrawal of the Mongols to contest the succession seemed to have saved a disunited Europe from complete destruction.

Ogedei had pursued the conquests begun by his father, Genghis Khan. He had pressed home the Mongol invasions in northern China and in Persia and Afghanistan. He had subdued Central Russia. By 1240, he was planning a western campaign against the plains of Hungary, which would supply rich pasturage for his Mongol horsemen and which contained the only branch of the Turco-Mongolian race outside Ogedei's Khanship. Some said that he planned an invasion throughout western Europe. Others believed that Hungary was the natural boundary for his vast empire.

The campaign in the west was master-minded by Subedei, a brilliant general and a veteran of the campaigns of Genghis Khan. He secured his lines of communication through Russia by the destruction of Kiev in 1240. Early in the following year, he gathered his forces around Przemsyl, on the border between Poland and what is now the Soviet Union. From there, he divided his force into four groups. One went north, under the command of Prince Kaidu, to protect the right flank of the main army and to forestall any attack from central Europe.

	Mongol cavalry
	Henry of Silesia
	Bela of Hungary
	cavalry

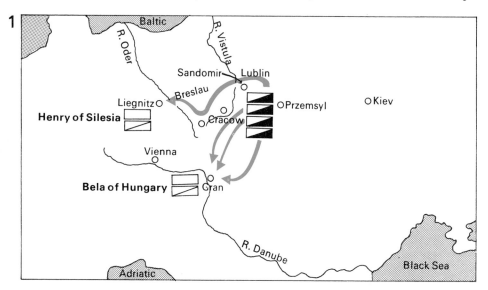

Advancing from Kiev to Przemsyl, the Mongols press on westwards. Kaidu rides north and defeats the Germans outside Liegnitz. Subedei divides the rest of his force in three and prepares to advance on the Hungarians at Gran.

Asian heavy cavalry in combat at about the time of Mohi Heath. Near-contemporary illustrations of soldiers of this period often show very different styles of armour.

The other three forces prepared to attack the main objective, the plains of Hungary and the Hungarian army under King Bela IV (Plan 1).

Each force consisted of about three toumans, each of about 10,000 horsemen. In the strictly organized and highly disciplined Mongol army, the touman often acted as an independent force, made up of regiments, companies and platoons, each of ten units. The toumans could also act with remarkable co-ordination, thanks to the efficient Mongol system of signalling, which included flaming arrows at night and black and white flags in the day. This allowed precise and silent communication over both long and short distances that was a great deal faster than a messenger could move on horseback. Subedei's wide use of spies also enabled him to plan well ahead in the full knowledge of the enemy's movements.

All Mongol soldiers were mounted. They only dismounted to fight in exceptional circumstances. It was far easier for the Mongols to operate with a single arm than for the Hungarians to co-ordinate a force of infantry and cavalry which often operated with little regard for each other. Mongol horsemen were, however, divided into two main types: heavier 'shock' troops, armed with lances and protected by armour composed of pieces of tanned hide arranged in overlapping plates that were lacquered for waterproofing; and light, un-armoured troops, armed with javelins, bows and three types of arrows for penetrating various degrees of armour. All troops carried their personal necessities with them. The horses were small and sturdy, carefully trained, and equipped with a stirrup that enabled the rider to fire accurately at a gallop.

Mongol tactics softened up the enemy with the firepower of the light cavalry before attacking with the heavy cavalry. The heavy cavalry usually faced the enemy, allowing gaps in their ranks through which the light horsemen could advance, fire and then retreat. When confronted by a large force, the Mongols did not attempt to bring about a major action. They preferred to retreat, harassing the enemy with arrows and javelins, until their opponents were tired out. Even then, when they launched their attack, they rarely attempted to conclude a decisive engagement on the battlefield itself, where the enemy would be forced to fight with the energy of despair. It was more economical of Mongol manpower to encourage the enemy to escape through a prepared avenue so that

they could be ridden down as they fled and slaughtered with great ease.

It was with such an army that Subedei invaded eastern Europe, choosing the winter months when the frozen conditions made river-crossing easier. Kaidu advanced rapidly through Lublin and across the Vistula. He sacked Sandomir and burnt Cracow. Then he crossed the Oder, threatened Breslau and met the German forces under Duke Henry of Silesia outside Liegnitz on April 8, 1241 (Plan 1). Kaidu attacked Duke Henry the following day, before he could be reinforced by King Wenceslas of Bohemia, who was only 24 hours away. Duke Henry was slain and his army slaughtered. Nine sackfuls of right ears were sent to Prince Batu, nominal commander of the invading forces. Kaidu then turned south to join Batu and Subedei.

Subedei achieved his own objective almost simultaneously. He destroyed the Hungarian army at Mohi Heath on April 10, the day after Kaidu's victory. He had been cautious as well as bold, not relying entirely on Kaidu to protect his right flank. Two of his three remaining groups, advancing from Przemsyl, had made wide sweeps to the north and south, while the central one, under his command, hung back at first and then made a rapid advance directly ahead (Plan 1). The van of this central group travelled 180 miles (290 kilometres) in

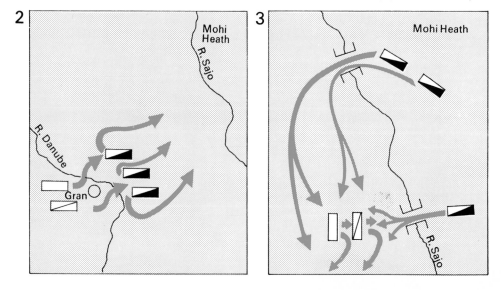

*Far left: The Hungarians
fall for the bait and cross the
Danube to pursue the
retreating Mongols through
the snow towards the River
Sajo and Mohi Heath.*

*Left: Batu attacks the
Hungarians across the bridge
and holds their attention
while Subedei crosses unseen
by a ford and launches a
surprise attack on the
Hungarian flank and rear.
True to style the Mongols
leave the Hungarians an
avenue of escape so they can
be slaughtered more easily.*

Single combat between Asian horsemen, riding out in front of their respective armies.

three days through snow and across ice. With perfectly planned co-ordination, the three groups met on the Danube, near the Hungarian capital of Gran. Across the river, King Bela had collected an army of 100,000, greater in fact than the force under Subedei and Batu. Subedei decided that it was unwise to attempt to cross the river under the eyes of the enemy and unsafe, even if he did so, to fight with his back to the Danube. On April 4, he therefore began a strategic retreat back the way he had just come. Bela could not resist the temptation to follow, as the Mongols had hoped. The retreat continued for six days and Bela's army was drawn even deeper into the snow and ice to the east of the Danube (Plan 2).

On the sixth day, the Mongols reached the River Sajo, where there was a bridge and a ford further upstream, as Subedei discovered by a reconnoitre. The Mongols encamped on the far side of the river, on Mohi Heath, on the evening of April 9. That night, Subedei took part of the force and crossed by the ford, unknown to King Bela. Batu seized the bridge in the morning and attacked the front of the Hungarian army. Bela believed that he was facing the entire Mongol horde and committed himself wholly to this front (Plan 3).

He was completely taken by surprise when Subedei appeared on his flank and rear. Crushed together, Bela's soldiers quickly panicked. The Mongols left an avenue of escape, true to their usual tactics, and in three days of continuous pursuit 70,000 Hungarians and allies were killed. According to an eye-witness, 'their bodies were strewn everywhere like stones in a quarry'. The strategic withdrawal, tactical envelopment and traditional tactical manoeuvres of the Mongols, had given Subedei one of his most convincing victories.

Subedei (c.1164–1250)

One of the leading Mongol generals when he was only 25, Subedei helped to spread the empire of Genghis Khan from Northern China to the Black Sea. He reappeared in the west under Ogedei Khan and smashed the Hungarians at Mohi Heath (sometimes known as the Battle of Sajo River). Europe could have offered little resistance had he decided to advance still further. Subedei retired at 80, in 1244/45, to his home pastures in Kerulen, leaving the battlefields and the Mongol Court at Karakoram, to die alone in the steppes. His combination of swift action, mobility and understanding of the fluctuating fortunes of every battle won him more than sixty victories during his long life and enabled him to conquer more than thirty nations.

Tannenberg 1914

Total encirclement of the enemy is the ultimate tactical achievement. The Mongols were in a position to accomplish this at Mohi Heath but refrained in favour of the richer rewards of a slaughterous pursuit. In modern times, the Germans very nearly closed the net on the Russians at Tannenberg. Two senior officers, Hoffman and von Francois, anticipated their commanders' plan, risked leaving one Russian army unguarded and enveloped Samsonov's Second Army in preparation for the 'Day of Harvesting'.

Tannenberg had been the scene of a disastrous defeat suffered by the Teutonic knights in the 15th Century. More than 500 years later a German army erased the memory of that defeat by winning a classic victory against the Russians. Just as the original battle became part of the

Teutonic saga, so the 20th-Century battle quickly gathered about itself the aura of myth. Victory was credited to an ageing but admirable general brought out of retirement to complete his life's ambition of pushing the Russians into the Masurian Lakes and to the brilliant plan of his Chief of Staff. The two men were Paul von Hindenburg and Erich Ludendorff. Certainly, they bore responsibility for the battle but the credit should have gone to the clear thinking of a young Operations Staff officer, Colonel Max Hoffman, and the decisive and energetic action of a corps commander, Herman von Francois, who several times disregarded Ludendorff's dithering and contradictory orders to fulfil the spirit of Hoffman's planning.

The German offensive in the west in the opening weeks of the First World War had at first been swift. It was slowing down by August but the prolonged deadlock that characterized much of the war was not reached until after the Battle of the Marne had halted the German advance for good. The Battle of the Marne was not concluded until two weeks after the Battle of Tannenberg. Meanwhile, the German commander in the west still had faint hopes of achieving victory within the year. The French, too, were quite prepared to believe in the possibility of an immediate German victory and had urged Tsar Nicolas II of Russia to mobilize his forces at once and to attack the Germans in East Prussia. The Russians were disorganized, badly staffed and thoroughly unprepared but the Tsar was eager to give loyal support to his allies. Two armies were dispatched under the overall command of General Jilinsky. The Russian First Army, under General Rennenkampf, was to advance north of the Masurian Lakes, through Gumbinnen. The Second Army, under General Samsonov, was to advance further south and come up towards Soldau. The intention was to create a pincer movement that would grip the German Eighth Army, under General von Prittwitz (Plan 1).

Rennenkampf and Samsonov were old arch-rivals and Jilinsky had insufficient control over them. They advanced with virtually no co-ordination and gradually drew further and further apart. The Masurian Lakes stood between them so that, even had they wanted to, they could give each other little support. Their advances were also quite different in character. Rennenkampf's natural caution slowed him down, while Samsonov's eagerness drove him forward, despite increasing lack of supplies, appallingly sandy country and an inadequate system of communications and transport, all of which left his troops exhausted for the coming battle.

Leaving XX Corps under Scholtz, to conduct a holding operation to the west of Samsonov, Prittwitz decided to concentrate his main force against Rennenkampf (Plan 2). The first engagement took place on August 17, at Stalluponen, where the overwhelming Russian numbers were able to hold the vigorous attack by von Francois's I Corps. A further engagement occurred at Gumbinnen three days later. Von Francois was supported by I Corps reserve, under Otto von Below, and XVII Corps, under von Mackensen. Fortunes varied across the battlefield and the result of this encounter, on August 20, was more or less even. Rennenkampf came to standstill and the Germans withdrew again.

The German setbacks had not been great but Prittwitz was as nervous as Rennenkampf. His fears were increased when he learnt that Samsonov, encouraged by Jilinsky, had pushed forward to make contact with Scholtz's XX Corps. Despite the protestations of the Operations Staff, including Hoffman, the jittery Prittwitz decided to retreat behind the safe line of the River Vistula, to the west. This had been the plan, worked out before the war, in the event of a Russian offensive gaining the initiative. Prittwitz telegrammed his decision to von Moltke and demanded reinforcements to help him hold the line of the Vistula. Von Moltke had his own problems in the west but acted quickly. He detached two corps and sent them east, although they did not in fact arrive on the eastern front in time for the coming battle. He also dismissed Prittwitz

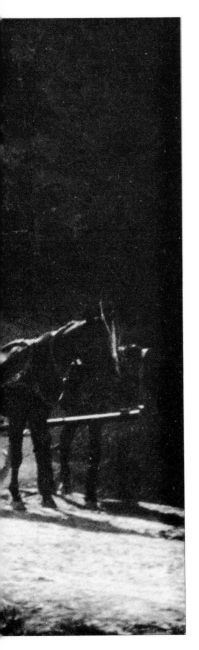

Left: Max Hoffman, when he later became Chief of Staff in the East. He was a colonel at the time of Tannenberg.

German troops on the march on the Eastern front. The long columns kicked up clouds of dust as soon as the Spring mud had dried.

and replaced him by Ludendorff, who had a proven record of success. As a gesture of caution, he recalled the steadfast Hindenburg from retirement to act as Ludendorff's nominal commander-in-chief.

Ludendorff hastened by train to the east, pausing only to pick up his commander at Hanover station. It was in the train journey to their new command that the two men discussed their plan for dealing with the combined Russian armies but, when they arrived at the front on August 23, they found that Hoffman had already conceived a similar plan and had initiated the moves necessary to fulfil it. The plan relied on Rennenkampf staying where he was and making no move to go to the assistance of Samsonov. It was not an unreasonable hypothesis. A small German force would remain to keep an eye on Rennenkampf while the main German attack was made against the Russian Second Army. One cavalry division was left in the north; several more divisions went to the aid of Scholtz in the centre; Below and Mackensen started off by road to attack the right wing of Samsonov's army; and von Francois set off on a roundabout route by rail to attack the Russian left wing (Plan 3). The entire plan was basically conceived to stop Samsonov from advancing any further. The risk was that Rennenkampf might move suddenly to attack the rear of the German army. It was a calculated risk and there were several factors that weighed in its favour. Below and Mackensen found it hard enough to cover the distance by road between the two armies; in theory, Rennenkampf would find it even harder to circle the Masurian Lakes. It was also well known that Rennenkampf would be in no hurry to help Samsonov and, from orders found on a captured Russian officer, it was confirmed that Rennenkampf had no immediate plans to move on from his present position.

The German manoeuvres took several days, during which Samsonov seemed unaware of the impending peril. He pressed forward his attack on Scholtz in the centre on August 24 and 25 and steadily pushed back XX Corps. As soon as von Francois arrived, via Konigsberg, Marienburg and Deutsch Eylau, he was ordered by Ludendorff to go immediately into battle on Scholtz's right wing and not to continue his flanking move round Soldau to Neidenberg. Von Francois claimed that his artillery had not yet caught up with him and refused to obey Ludendorff. He pressed forward with the original plan, knowing that Samsonov's army would slip away to the south-east if he did not do so.

The Russian right wing had become slightly detached from the main army and Mackensen and Below came up against them on August 26. The Russians were turned back in considerable confusion after a fierce engagement. The Germans continued their advance through Passenheim. On August 27, two of

Germans ▮ cavalry ◣
Russians ☐

The two Russian armies attempt a pincer movement to cut off von Prittwitz's Eighth Army. Rennenkampf's First Army advances to the north of the Masurian Lakes while Samsonov's Second Army makes faster progress to the south.

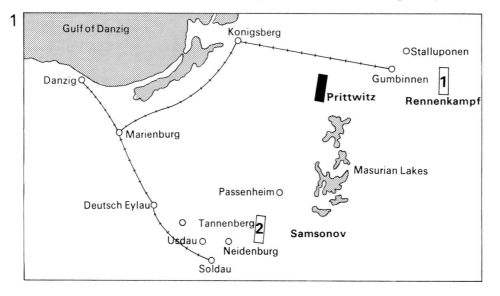

Russian prisoners of war taken by the Germans after the Battle of Tannenberg. About 90,000 prisoners were taken altogether on the 'Day of Harvesting'.

Samsonov's corps, under Martov and Kliuviev, made a concerted attack in the centre, which was once again valiantly held by Scholtz. At the same time, von Francois opened up with a heavy bombardment from Usdau. Samsonov himself came up from Neidenberg on August 27 to direct the attack and Ludendorff, beginning to panic, again ordered von Francois to go to Scholtz's aid. Simply ignoring the order this time, von Francois continued his advance towards Neidenberg, for the disenchanted Russians were already retreating through Tannenberg and the densely wooded country behind. With Mackensen and Below pressing down on the Russian right and Scholtz still holding in

Scholtz is left with XX Corps to hold Samsonov's Second Army while the bulk of the German Eighth Army advances against the Russian First Army. The German I Corps and XVII Corps undertake the first engagements with the Russians.

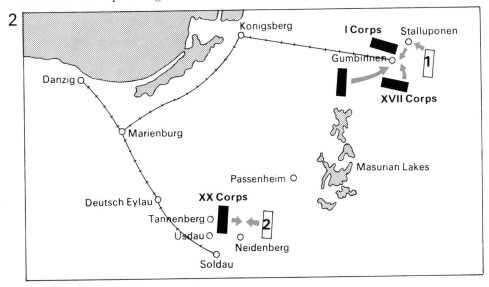

the centre, von Francois was anxious to catch the Russians on the left and in their rear. The net was closing in (Plan 4).

It was only then that Jilinsky realized the seriousness of the situation and ordered Rennenkampf to move south to help Samsonov. Rennenkampf moved with anxious slowness in the wrong direction. Instead of going south-west, he marched directly west. By the evening of August 29, the battle was decided. Von Francois had seized the road between Neidenberg and Willenberg and hemmed in the struggling fugitives from the Russian centre and left. In the confusion, Samsonov walked off alone into the wood and never reappeared. It was assumed that he shot himself.

Despite von Francois's desperate attempts to ignore Ludendorff's frustrating series of orders and to close the net to the south-east to trap the escaping Russians, the ring was not in fact as complete as it might have been. Mackensen and Below failed to move fast enough to join up with von Francois behind the Russians. Their failure was not entirely their fault. Ludendorff had a hand in it. He was alarmed by the news that Rennenkampf was at last making a move (albeit in the wrong direction) and gave contradictory orders divided between guarding himself against attack from the north and completing the attack to the south. Although Mackensen did make last minute efforts to close the gap, many Russians escaped between his corps and that of von Francois.

It was panic as much as anything that ensured the fate of the remaining Russians. Von Francois himself rounded up 60,000 prisoners. In all, 90,000 prisoners were taken, including Martov and Kliuviev and almost three entire Russian corps. Thirty thousand more Russians were killed. August 30 and 31 became known as the 'Day of Harvesting'. German casualties totalled about 13,000.

Hindenburg and Ludendorff crowned their victory by turning north and attacking Rennenkampf in the second week of September. It was the culmination of Hoffman's original plan. They did not drive Rennenkampf into the sea, as they had hoped, nor did they shatter him quite as thoroughly as they had shattered Samsonov, but they inflicted a decisive defeat on him and drove him back into Russia at the Battle of the Masurian Lakes. This victory followed so closely on Tannenberg that German morale was raised to a high pitch and was able to ignore the considerable setback at the Marne in the west. The two defeats also destroyed the Allied confidence in the Russian armies. The Russians did in fact recover to invade East Prussia once again but their early defeats greatly prolonged the war. If they had won, the Germans would have been sorely pressed in the autumn and winter of 1914 and might well have

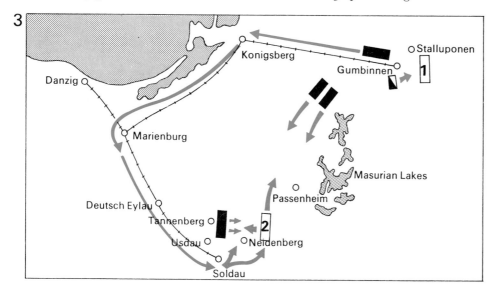

While Scholtz continues to hold Samsonov, I Corps Reserve and XVII Corps head south to take Samsonov's northern flank while von Francois takes the long rail route round to Samsonov's southern flank. One cavalry division is left to guard Rennenkampf in the north.

Russian infantry on the march, heading west to meet the Germans in the opening campaign of the First World War. Their order contrasts with that of their opponents a few pages back.

succumbed to the double pressure from east and west.

The German victory at Tannenberg was aided by the incompetence and tiredness of the Russian troops. It was also won very largely in spite of the presence of the two German overall commanders. Hoffman's carefully balanced plan was perfectly complemented by the energy and resolve of von Francois, who was determined not to be distracted from his purpose. The result was a classic victory of double envelopment.

Hermann von Francois *(1856–1933)*

A German field commander of enormous potential, von Francois was held back by the not inconsiderable jealousy of Ludendorff, who ensured that he never rose above the rank of corps commander. The victory at Tannenberg was made convincing by his single-minded determination to cut off the Russian line of retreat.

Max Hoffman *(1869–1927)*

A brilliant German staff officer, who advised Hindenburg and Ludendorff in their eastern operations and subsequently became Chief of Staff in the east, Hoffman also helped to draw up the Brest-Litovsk agreement with the Bolsheviks. He provided the plan which determined the successful action at Tannenberg, although Ludendorff claimed the entire credit.

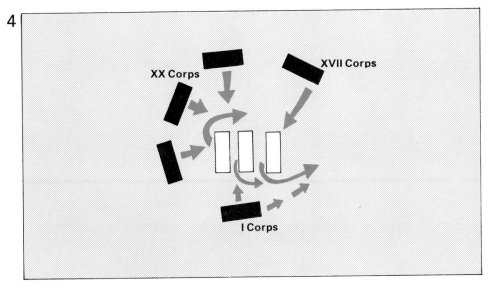

The final encirclement of Samsonov's Second Army. The net is not quite closed to the east and many Russians escaped the 'Day of Harvesting'.

The double envelopment that was achieved at Tannenberg has often been hailed as a modern Cannae. That Roman disaster still remains war's most perfect example of total encirclement—a tactical masterpiece. Hannibal used both cunning and active leadership to lure the Romans forward into a compact and helpless mass on an open plain. When his infantry turned against the Roman flanks and his cavalry hit them from behind, seven out of eight legions were annihilated. No victory has ever been so complete.

A silver triple shekel bearing what is generally considered to be the portrait head of Hannibal. This coin was struck in Spain by the Barcids about 237–218 BC. (By kind permission of the Trustees of the British Museum)

The Carthaginians took the Romans by storm when they crossed the Alps in 218 BC. Hannibal established his supremacy in the Po valley and invaded the boot of Italy the next year, defeating all Roman forces sent against him. Not yet ready to attack Rome itself, he preferred to play for time and to persuade Rome's Italian confederates to join his side. The Roman Senate determined on a knock-out blow and doubled the normal military establishment of four legions. They sent the reinforcements into Apulia to join the army (under the consuls Paulus and Varro) that was harassing Hannibal. Meanwhile the Carthaginians encamped near the citadel of Cannae, on the right bank of the River Aufidus, which flowed north-east into the Adriatic, about six miles (9.6 kilometres) away. Although Cannae itself was on a hill forming part of a low spur running down the right-hand bank of the Aufidus, the terrain was mostly a low coastal plain. The river was easily fordable, not a major obstacle.

The Roman army, with its establishment doubled, consisted of eight legions, each composed, with allies, of about 10,000 infantry. Most of these were heavy infantry, equipped with body armour, shields, spears and short swords. They were drilled to fight shoulder-to-shoulder in serried ranks. The rest were light infantry, or velites, who wore no body armour but had shields, helmets, javelins and swords. These were recruited from among the younger men and were intended to supply the speed lacking in the heavy infantry. The Romans also had 6000 cavalry, heavily armoured but generally less effective than horsemen from nomadic or semi-nomadic barbarian tribes.

Hannibal's light infantry, without body armour, consisted of 20,000 Gauls and Spaniards. His heavy infantry was a body of 12,000 Libyans, who were roughly comparable to their Roman equivalents and who were largely equipped with captured Roman armour. Balearic slingers and spearmen made up

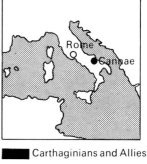

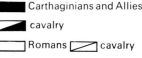
Carthaginians and Allies
cavalry
Romans / cavalry

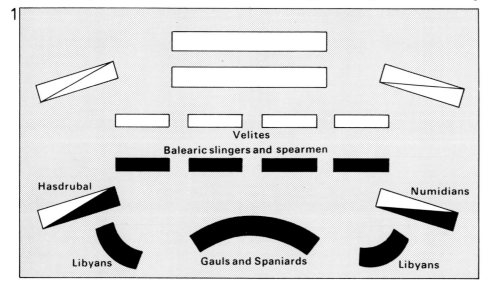

1

Velites
Balearic slingers and spearmen
Hasdrubal
Numidians
Libyans
Gauls and Spaniards
Libyans

The conventional line-up of the Roman legions is faced by the more imaginative disposition of Hannibal's forces. Both sides are fronted by a thin line of skirmishers.

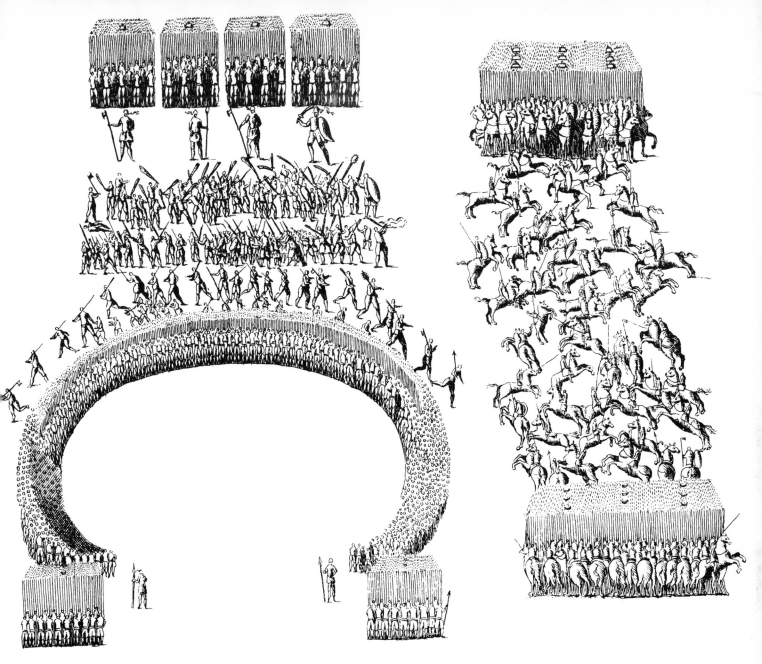

the bulk of another 8000 light troops, giving a total of 40,000 infantry as against 80,000 Roman infantry. The Carthaginian cavalry was stronger than its Roman equivalent: 10,000 as against 6000. There were heavily armed Iberian and Gallic horsemen and light, irregular Numidians.

The Romans detached one legion to defend their own camps and to create a side show by attacking the Carthaginian camp. They then drew up their line of battle, facing south, with its right wing on the Aufidus. Hannibal detached rather fewer men for much the same purpose and faced north. Both sides fronted their lines with the conventional thin veneer of skirmishers. These were velites in the case of the Romans and Balearic slingers and spearmen in the case of the Carthaginians.

The main line of the Roman army was drawn up according to standard Roman practice, in a straight line, with the cavalry and some light infantry on either wing and the heavy infantry massed in the centre (Plan 1). They intended to rely on the superiority of their infantry to break up the Carthaginians. But in so doing they made a grave mistake. They were accustomed to a military establishment of four legions, which they usually deployed over a front of 1500 yards (1370 metres). With an extra four legions on this occasion (less one detached), they had a rare opportunity to double their front. If they had done so, Hannibal would have had to spread his own line dangerously thin and the Romans might have had the chance to envelop the Carthaginian wings or break through their line. Instead, they retained their customary front and merely doubled its depth, putting their trust in tradition and sheer weight.

Hannibal could not hope to defeat the Romans by a frontal assault. He was bound to base himself on his cavalry superiority and attempt to turn one or other of the Roman flanks. He decided to turn both. His plan was daringly conceived and perfectly matched to the situation and to the Roman mentality. His problem was how to hold the Roman infantry while his cavalry accomplished their attack. His solution was to form his Gauls and Spaniards, his light infantry, into a crescent projecting towards the centre of the Roman lines. At either end of the crescent he placed 6000 Libyan heavy infantry in line. These two units would provide the only stable position in a battle line that otherwise would be in a state of permanent flux. Beyond the Libyans, on his left, he placed the Gallic-Iberian heavy cavalry, under his brother Hasdrubal, and on the right he placed the light Numidian horse, under Hanno.

The crescent was a calculated risk. An oblique attack by the Romans, or even an attack in depth on both sides to pinch out the salient, would put an end to his hopes. But Hannibal trusted that the Romans would advance in a precisely straight line. They would then encounter the centre of the crescent, which they would drive back inevitably. As they did so, the crescent would shorten and thicken, reinforced not by reserves but by the sheer logic of geometry. The longer it took the Romans to drive in the crescent, the greater the time for the cavalry to encircle the enemy.

The initial encounter between the skirmishing troops was indecisive. Hannibal then ordered forward his two cavalry wings, each against its Roman equivalent, while the solid line of the Roman infantry clanked inexorably towards the Carthaginian crescent. Hasdrubal's cavalry fell upon the Roman right wing in earnest, not hesitating where necessary to descend to fight on foot. Those Romans who escaped death on the spot were pursued along the banks of the river. Things did not go so well for the Carthaginians on the Roman left wing. The Numidian light cavalry were accustomed to hit and run tactics. They failed to break the Roman cavalry and resorted to constant harassment to prevent the Romans from being effectively engaged in the battle.

Meanwhile the Roman line encountered the centre of Hannibal's crescent and faced their first problem. While the centre of the Roman line engaged the centre of the crescent, the legions at either end found themselves suspended

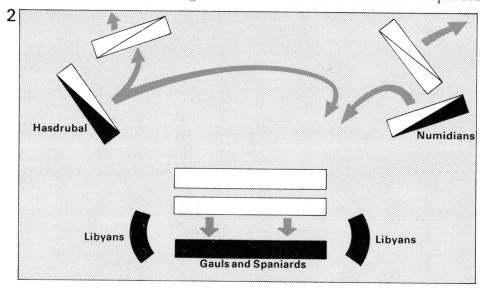

2

Hasdrubal

Numidians

Libyans

Libyans

Gauls and Spaniards

The Roman infantry close their ranks to squeeze between Hannibal's heavy Libyan infantry. The convex centre of Hannibal's line is gradually forced back. Meanwhile, Hasdrubal's left wing cavalry have driven off their opposite numbers and have crossed the battlefield to help the Numidian cavalry of the right wing. Together both forces of cavalry turn to attack the Roman rear.

The obverse of the silver denarius on the opposite page. It shows a portrait of the goddess Roma. (By kind permission of the Trustees of the British Museum)

without an opponent. Rather than lose their straight line and attack the flank of the crescent, they closed up laterally towards the centre. The entire Roman front would now pass between the Carthaginian heavy infantry pivots (Plan 2).

Hannibal himself was fighting amongst the heroically resisting Gauls and Spaniards, to rally them against the remorseless pressure of the Roman front. Steadily, Roman weight told and the bulge of the crescent was eliminated until it began to sag in the opposite direction between the two units of the heavy infantry. From now on the logic of geometry would be against the Carthaginians. Hannibal ordered the Libyans to attack the Roman flanks.

The cavalry battle in the rear had turned on the intelligent movement of Hasdrubal, who had broken off his pursuit of the Roman cavalry on the right and had ridden across to the Roman left to locate the Numidians before completing his orders to attack the Roman rear. Together, both lots of cavalry dismissed their opponents on the Roman left and fell on the Roman rear. The encirclement of the Roman army was complete (Plan 3).

The effect was dramatic. The Roman advance against the Carthaginian light infantry ground to a halt. The Libyan heavy infantry further compressed the Roman ranks, and the legions became so tightly packed that there was no longer room for any unit to build up enough momentum to break out nor for the survivors of the mauled ranks to let fresh men through to the front. The result was the virtual annihilation of the Roman army. Of the 6000 Roman horse, only 370 escaped, along with the consul Varro, whose turn it had been to command that day (the consuls took alternate days). Paulus and 70,000 legionaries were slaughtered and all but 3000 of the rest were taken prisoner. Cannae became a byword for disaster. It was also the ultimate tactical triumph.

Hannibal *(247–183/2 BC)*

Accused by the Romans of cruelty, avarice and treachery, Hannibal was certainly courageous, a powerful leader of men and one of the greatest military commanders of the past. The Romans themselves were forced to admire his tactical brilliance in the field and the speed with which he marched up and down Italy. After campaigning successfully in Spain and marching through Gaul, he achieved his best-known feat of crossing the Alps to fall 'like a thunderbolt' on northern Italy. He failed to follow up his victory at Cannae and to attack Rome because he lacked the siege equipment to do so. After many years harassing the Romans, his Carthaginian army was finally defeated at Zama, in 202 BC. Hannibal survived for another 20 years but was finally exiled and poisoned himself to escape arrest by the Romans.

The Libyans close in on the Roman flanks, Hasdrubal attacks the Roman rear and Hannibal's threatened centre revives its resistance. The Roman legions are encompassed on all four sides. There is no escape.

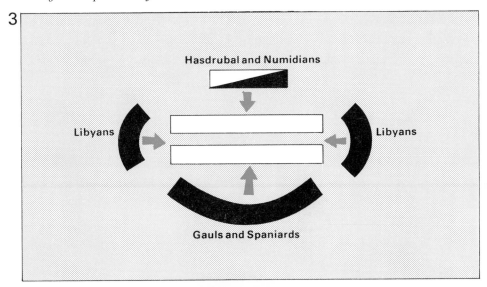

Bibliography

Arrian, trans. Sélingcourt A. de, *The Campaigns of Alexander*, 1972
Beer, Sir Gavin de, *Hannibal*, 1969
Belloc, H., *The Tactics and Strategy of the Great Duke of Marlborough*, 1933
Boudet, J., *The Ancient Art of Warfare* (2 vols.), 1969
Brett-James, A., *Wellington at War 1794–1815*, 1969
Brogan, Hugh (Ed.), *The American Civil War, Extracts from The Times 1860–1865*, 1975
Browning, Robert, *Justinian and Theodora*, 1971
Burn, A. R., *The Warring States of Greece*, 1968
Caesar, Julius, trans. Mitchell, Jane, *Civil Wars*, 1967
Chandler, D. C. (Ed.), *A Traveller's Guide to the Battlefields of Europe* (2 vols.), 1965
   The Art of Warfare on Land, 1974
   The Art of Warfare in the Age of Marlborough, 1976
Churchill, W. S., *Marlborough, His Life and Times*, 1933
Clark, Sir George, *The Seventeenth Century*, 1929
Clausewitz, Karl Von, *On War*, 1835
Davies, Norman, *White Eagle and Red Star, the Polish Soviet War 1919–1920*, 1972
Dexter, David, *The New Guinea Offensive*, 1961
Eisenschmil, Otto and Newman, Ralph, *The Civil War*, 1956
Evans, Geoffrey, *Slim as Military Commander*, 1969
Falls, Cyril (Ed.), *Great Military Battles*, 1964
Frankland and Dowling, *Decisive Battles of the Twentieth Century*, 1976
Fuller, J. F. C., *The Decisive Battles of the Western World* (3 vols.), 1954–1956
   The Generalship of Alexander the Great, 1958
   Julius Caesar, 1965
Guderian, H., *Panzer Leader*, 1952
Hammond, N. G. L., *A History of Greece to 332 B.C.*, 1959
Herodotus, trans. Sélingcourt A. de, *The Histories*, 1954
Jackson, W. G. F., *The North African Campaign 1940–1943*, 1975

Keegan and Wheatcroft, *Who's Who in Military History*, 1976
Legg, Stuart, *The Heartland*, 1970
Lewin, Ronald, *Montgomery as Military Commander*, 1971
Liddell Hart, B. H., *Great Captains Unveiled*, 1927
   History of the First World War, 1930
   History of the Second World War, 1970
   Strategy, The Indirect Approach, 1954
Marshall, James, *Napoleon as Military Commander*, 1967
Maule, Henry, *The Great Battles of World War Two*, 1972
Montet, Pierre, *Lives of the Pharaohs*, 1968
Montgomery, B. L., *A Concise History of Warfare*, 1972
   El Alamein to the River Sangro, 1946
Oman, C. W. C., *The Art of War in the Sixteenth Century*, 1937
   A History of the Art of War in the Middle Ages, 1924
Palit, D. K., *Return to Sinai 1973*, 1974
Pitt, Barrie (Ed.), *Great Battles of the Twentieth Century*, 1977
Plutarch, trans. Scott-Kilvert, I., *The Rise and Fall of Athens*, 1960
Procopius, trans. Dewing, H. B., *A History of the Wars*, 1928
Rhodes, James Ford, *History of the Civil War*, 1914
Ritter, G., *Frederick the Great*, 1968
Roberts, M., *The Military Revolution 1560–1660*, 1956
Saunders, J. J., *The History of the Mongol Conquests*, 1971
Sixsmith, Major, *British Generals of the Twentieth Century*, 1970
Slim, W., *Defeat into Victory*, 1956
Sunday Times Insight Team, *The Yom Kippur War*, 1975
Taylor, A. J. P., *The First World War*, 1963
Thucydides, trans. Warner, R., *A History of the Peloponnesian War*, 1954
Warner, Oliver, *Nelson's Battles*, 1965
Warner, Philip, *British Battlefields: The South*, 1972
Wedgwood, C. V., *The Thirty Years War*, 1938
Weller, J. A., *Weapons and Tactics*, 1966
Young, Brig. P., *A Dictionary of Battles 1816–1976*, 1977

ACKNOWLEDGEMENTS

The publishers would like to thank the following people and institutions for kind permission to use photographs and pictures:

Bibliothèque Nationale, Paris, and Mlle Gerin of the Cabinet de Médailles;
The British Museum, London, and Mr R. A. G. Carson, Keeper of Coins, Dept of Coins and Medals;
J. L. Englert;
Imperial War Museum, London;
The Mansell Collection;
The Parker Gallery, 2 Albemarle Street, London W1;
Phaidon Press Photographic Library;
Jozef Pilsudski Institute, London;
Rex Features Ltd;
Royal Asiatic Society;

General Sikorski Institute, London;
Spink & Son Ltd., London, with especial thanks to Mr G. E. Muller and Mr John Pett who also kindly arranged the photography of the British Museum material;
Sport & General;
Tower of London, Crown copyright reproduced with permission of the Controller of Her Majesty's Stationery Office;
The Wallace Collection, items reproduced by permission of the Trustees.

Research Assistant: Julia Schottlander
Diagrams drawn by David Parr
Cover Jacket by Carlo Tora photographed by Christopher Ridley

Index